A Blueprint for Production-Ready Web Applications

Leverage industry best practices to create complete web apps with Python, TypeScript, and AWS

Dr. Philip Jones

BIRMINGHAM—MUMBAI

A Blueprint for Production-Ready Web Applications

Group Product Manager: Pavan Ramchandani

Senior Editor: Hayden Edwards

Technical Editor: Simran Udasi

Copy Editor: Safis Editing

Project Coordinator: Sonam Pandey

Proofreader: Safis Editing

Indexer: Pratik Shirodkar

Production Designer: Roshan Kawale

Marketing Coordinators: Anamika Singh and Marylou De Mello

First published: September 2022

Production reference: 2010922

Published by Packt Publishing Ltd.

Livery Place

35 Livery Street

Birmingham

B3 2PB, UK.

978-1-80324-850-9

www.packt.com

Contributors

About the author

Dr. Philip Jones began his career studying physics at the University of Oxford, where he undertook his undergraduate studies and subsequently gained a doctorate in particle physics. He has authored the Quart framework, maintains the Flask framework, and supports the ongoing development of a number of other projects related to the Python HTTP stack. Currently, he works as a chief technical officer in London, and in his spare time, you will find him cycling or walking his dog, Penny.

I would like to thank my friends and family for their continued support and encouragement throughout the process of writing this book.

About the reviewers

Sunil Kumar is a passionate and energetic young man who is following his dream of changing the world with technology. He graduated from one of the top engineering colleges in India with a BTech degree in computer science and has years of profession experience. This experience includes backend development using Quart and Flask frameworks, and frontend development using ReactJS, along with queuing systems such as Kafka and RabbitMQ. Nowadays, he's working with FinTech companies helping to drive the change in the Indian economy and rethink debt collection systems.

Dr. Murray Hoggett worked in academia for 10 years researching climate change and volcanoes, specializing in numerical and stochastic simulations. Since then, he has worked as a software engineer on projects ranging from embedded systems and native apps to web apps and ML systems. He is currently team lead at TrueCircle, building Python and JavaScript web apps for the recycling industry.

Matt Dawson got his start in the tech industry working as a photographer/surveyor for a PropTech start-up. He developed an interest in engineering, and after graduating from Maker's Academy, he took a job as a full-stack engineer specializing in Python and TypeScript.

He now works as an infrastructure engineer, seeking a better understanding of how to deploy and scale applications that he was already able to build. He chose this due to his desire to understand the product as a whole, building on his strong foundation in backend/frontend principles.

Matt's love of tech is drawn from a strong curiosity to try new things and to constantly strive toward new levels of understanding, as well as his firm belief that anything can be made better.

Manuela Redinciuc is a full-stack software engineer from London, currently focusing on expanding her backend expertise at Lifeworks. She comes from a non-technical background and enjoys mentoring and helping others transition into tech roles.

Dr. Stuart Hannah is a professional software engineer living and working in London. He has extensive Python experience, holds a Ph.D. in combinatorics from Strathclyde University, and enjoys working on performant distributed systems.

Table of Contents

Part 2 Building a To-Do App

2

Creating a Reusable Backend with Quart   31

3

Building the API   59

4

Creating a Reusable Frontend with React   99

5

Building the Single-Page App   139

Part 3 Releasing a Production-Ready App

6

7

Preface

The aim of this book is to show you how to develop a web application using industry best practices and place it in a running production environment. We'll do this by creating a working to-do app. This app is live at `tozo.dev`, and all the code for it is available under the MIT license at `github.com/pgjones/tozo`.

The development blueprint presented in this book is based on one I've used to successfully build apps before, including for my own start-up a few years ago. The technology used here has been chosen because of its popularity in the industry, with Python, NodeJS, and Terraform being popular tools for full-stack development, and AWS being a popular cloud infrastructure provider.

I started writing this book as the guide I wish I'd had when I started my full-stack engineering career. I've tried to answer as many of the questions that I had when I started and introduce much of the vocabulary I was missing. Over the past year, I've been refining and using this blueprint to help guide and develop junior engineers in their first industrial jobs. I hope it helps you to build great apps too!

Who this book is for

This book is for software engineers who already know how to program (such as recent computer science or bootcamp graduates) and want to learn how to build an app following industry processes (for example, using continuous integration and deployment).

You will need a working knowledge of TypeScript/JavaScript, Python, HTML, CSS, and SQL. Apart from that, you are expected to be new to Quart, React, AWS, and all other specific technologies and processes introduced in the book.

What this book covers

In *Chapter 1, Setting Up Our System for Development*, we'll set up everything needed to develop the app. This includes installing Python, Node.js, Terraform, and Git, along with the associated tooling for each.

In *Chapter 2, Creating a Reusable Backend with Quart*, we'll build a backend that can be used for any app, introducing elements such as authentication, protection, database connections, and email.

In *Chapter 3, Building the API*, we'll build a to-do tracking RESTful CRUD API that includes member and session management.

In *Chapter 4, Creating a Reusable Frontend with React*, we'll build a frontend that can be used for any app, while discussing routing, styled data entry (forms), state management, and toast feedback.

In *Chapter 5, Building the Single-Page App*, we'll build a to-do tracking user interface by creating pages that allow users to register and log in to our app, as well as to change and manage their passwords.

In *Chapter 6, Deploying and Monitoring Your Application*, we'll deploy the app to AWS running in Docker. Here, we will discuss how to set up a domain name, employ HTTPS, and monitor the app for errors.

In *Chapter 7, Securing and Packaging the App*, we'll adopt industry best practices to secure the app and package it for the app stores, which includes adding multi-factor authentication and meeting the requirements to be a progressive web app.

To get the most out of this book

You will need to be able to read and understand basic Python, TypeScript, HTML, and SQL. Everything else will be introduced in the book.

Software/hardware covered in the book	Operating system requirements
Python	Windows
TypeScript	macOS
Terraform	Linux
SQL	
HTML	

All the installation instructions are present in the book.

If you are using the digital version of this book, we advise you to type the code yourself or access the code from the book's GitHub repository (a link is available in the next section). Doing so will help you avoid any potential errors related to the copying and pasting of code.

Download the example code files

You can download the example code files for this book from GitHub at `https://github.com/pgjones/tozo`. If there's an update to the code, it will be updated in the GitHub repository.

We also have other code bundles from our rich catalog of books and videos available at `https://github.com/PacktPublishing/`. Check them out!

Download the color images

We also provide a PDF file that has color images of the screenshots and diagrams used in this book. You can download it here: `https://packt.link/18OWu`.

Access the Code in Action videos

You can find the CiA videos for this book here: `https://bit.ly/3PBCd6r`.

Conventions used

There are a number of text conventions used throughout this book.

`Code in text`: Indicates code words in text, database table names, folder names, filenames, file extensions, pathnames, dummy URLs, user input, and Twitter handles. Here is an example: "The `reminderName` string is a string that uniquely identifies the reminder within the scope of the contextual grain."

A block of code is set as follows:

```
class APIError(Exception):
    def __init__(self, status_code: int, code: str) -> None:
        self.status_code = status_code
        self.code = code
```

When we wish to draw your attention to a particular part of a code block, the relevant lines or items are set in bold:

```
public interface IHotelGrain : IGrainWithStringKey
    {
        <<Code removed for brevity>>
        public Task Subscribe(IObserver observer);
        public Task UnSubscribe(IObserver observer);
```

Any command-line input or output is written as follows:

```
az monitor app-insights component create --app ai-distel-prod
--location westus  --resource-group rg-distel-prod
```

Bold: Indicates a new term, an important word, or words that you see onscreen. For instance, words in menus or dialog boxes appear in **bold**. Here is an example: "The **Client System** sends the batches of messages to the **Dispatcher Grain**, which enumerates through the batch of messages to dispatch the messages to each target grain."

> **Tips or Important Notes**
> Appear like this.

Get in touch

Feedback from our readers is always welcome.

General feedback: If you have questions about any aspect of this book, email us at `customercare@packtpub.com` and mention the book title in the subject of your message.

Errata: Although we have taken every care to ensure the accuracy of our content, mistakes do happen. If you have found a mistake in this book, we would be grateful if you would report this to us. Please visit `www.packtpub.com/support/errata` and fill in the form.

Piracy: If you come across any illegal copies of our works in any form on the internet, we would be grateful if you would provide us with the location address or website name. Please contact us at `copyright@packt.com` with a link to the material.

If you are interested in becoming an author: If there is a topic that you have expertise in and you are interested in either writing or contributing to a book, please visit `authors.packtpub.com`.

Share Your Thoughts

Once you've read *A Blueprint for Production-Ready Web Applications*, we'd love to hear your thoughts! Scan the QR code below to go straight to the Amazon review page for this book and share your feedback.

`https://packt.link/r/1-803-24850-5`

Your review is important to us and the tech community and will help us make sure we're delivering excellent quality content.

Part 1
Setting Up Our System

Before we can build our app, we need a system that is set up for fast development. This means we'll need to install tooling to autoformat, lint, and test our code, alongside using Git for version control and Terraform to manage the infrastructure.

This part consists of the following chapter:

- *Chapter 1, Setting Up Our System for Development*

1
Setting Up Our System for Development

The aim of this book is to provide a blueprint for a web app running in a production environment and utilizing as many industrial best practices as possible. To do this, we will build a working to-do app, codenamed Tozo, that allows users to track a list of tasks. You can see the finished app in *Figure 1.1*:

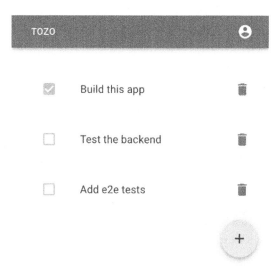

Figure 1.1: The to-do app we'll build in this book

While the aim is to build a working to-do app, we'll focus on features that are useful to any app, with much of the functionality and many of the techniques being the same as in the app built here. For example, users will need to log in, change their password, and so on. Therefore, my hope is that you can take this blueprint, remove the small amount of specific to-do code, and build your own app.

In this chapter, we will take a new machine without any tooling and set it up for development. We'll also set up systems to develop and test the app automatically. Specifically, we'll install a system package manager and use it to install the various language runtimes and tooling before setting up a remote repository and activating continuous integration. By the end of this chapter, you'll have everything you need to be able to focus solely on developing the app. This means that you will be able to quickly build and test the features you need in your app for your users.

So, in this chapter, we will cover the following topics:

- Aiming for fast development
- Setting up our system
- Installing Python for backend development
- Installing NodeJS for frontend development
- Installing Terraform for infrastructure development
- Installing PostgreSQL for database development
- Adopting a collaborative development process using GitHub

Technical requirements

I've built the app described in this book and you can use it by visiting the following link: `https://tozo.dev`. The code is also available at `https://github.com/pgjones/tozo` (feel free to use that code or the code in this book under the MIT license).

I'm going to assume you have a working knowledge of TypeScript and Python, as these are the languages we'll use to write the app. However, we're going to avoid any esoteric language features and I hope the code is easily understandable. I'm also going to assume you are happy using the command line, rather than focusing on GUI instructions, as most tooling is optimized for command-line usage, and this is something that should be advantageous.

To follow the development in this chapter, use the companion repository at `https://github.com/pgjones/tozo` and see the commits between the `r1-ch1-start` and `r1-ch1-end` tags.

Aiming for fast development

Before we start setting up our system to build the to-do app, it's important to understand what we are aiming for when building any app, which is to solve our customer's needs by shipping solutions as quickly as possible. This means that we must understand their needs, translate them into working code, and crucially, deploy the solution with confidence that it works as expected.

When we are developing an app, the shorter the time between making a change to the code and being able to run and see the effect of the change, the better. This is why we will run all of the code locally, with auto-reloading enabled; this should mean that any change we make is testable in our local browser within a few seconds.

> **Hot/auto-reloading**
>
> In development, we ideally want any changes we make to the code to take effect immediately so that we can check that the changes have the desired effect. This feature is called hot or auto-reloading and is active with the React and Quart development servers we are using in this book.

I also like to use tooling to help speed up development and gain confidence that the code works as expected. This tooling should run as frequently as possible, ideally as part of an automated process. I have split this tooling into auto-formatting, linting, and testing categories.

Auto-formatting the code

The format and style of code matter as a different style to the one you are used to will take longer for you to understand. This will mean more bugs as you spend more of your time comprehending the style rather than logic. Also, while you can be consistent, almost everyone has a different preferred style, and I've found that these preferences change over time.

In the past, I've used tooling to check the styling and report on any inconsistencies. This is helpful but wasteful as every inconsistency must be fixed manually. Fortunately, most languages now have an official, or dominant, **auto-formatter** that both defines a style and changes all of the code to match it. Using the most popular auto-formatter means that most developers will recognize your code.

We'll aim to set up our tooling so that there are auto-formatters for as much of the code as possible.

Linting the code

I think of **linting** in two parts: type checking and static analysis. Type checking requires that we include types when writing the code. I use type hinting, or typed languages, where possible, as this catches a large number of the errors I typically make. Typing also helps document the code, meaning that it makes it clear what objects (types) are expected. While typing costs more effort to write, I think it easily pays off in bugs avoided. Therefore, checking the typing should be our first aim of linting.

The second part, static analysis, allows linters to look for potential issues in naming, usage of functions, possible bugs, security issues, and unused code, and to flag code that is too complex or poorly constructed. These linters are a very low-cost sanity check as they are quick and easy to run and give few false issues (positives).

Testing the code

While linting will identify bugs and issues with the code, it cannot detect logical issues where correctly written code does the wrong thing. To identify these, we need to write tests that check that the execution of the code results in the expected output. Therefore, it is important that we write tests as we write the code, especially when we discover bugs. We will focus on writing tests that provide an easy way to test that the app works as expected.

> **Test coverage**
>
> Test coverage is used to measure how much of the code has been tested by the test suite. This is typically done by measuring the ratio of lines executed by the tests to the total lines of code. I find this metric unhelpful as it focuses on lines executed rather than use cases that matter to the user. Therefore, I'd encourage you to focus on testing the use cases you think your users require. However, if you'd like to measure coverage this way, you can install `pytest-cov` using `pdm`.

Using auto-formatters, linters, and a testing suite allows us to develop with greater confidence and therefore speed, which in turn means a better experience for our users. However, in order to use these tools, we will first need to set up our system effectively.

Setting up our system

To effectively develop our app, we will need to be able to develop and run it. This means we will need tooling to manage changes to the code, test and check the app for errors, and run it. This tooling can be installed via a system package manager, of which there are many choices depending on your operating system. I recommend that you install Homebrew on Linux (`https://linuxbrew.sh`) and macOS (`https://brew.sh`), or Scoop (`https://scoop.sh`) on Windows. I'll show both `brew` and `scoop` commands in this book, but you should only use the command that works on your operating system.

You will also need a code editor to write the code in and a browser to run the app. I recommend that you install VS Code (`https://code.visualstudio.com`) and Chrome (`https://www.google.com/chrome`) via the directions given on their websites. With these tools installed, we can now consider how we'll manage the code.

Managing the code

As we develop our app, we will inevitably make mistakes and want to return to the previous working version. You may also want to share the code with others, or just keep a backup for yourself. This is why we need to manage the code via a **version control** system. While there are many different version control systems, the majority in this industry use git (`https://git-scm.com`). It can be installed via the system package manager as follows:

```
brew install git
scoop install git
```

> **Using git**
>
> This book can be completed using `git add` to add files to the repository, `git commit` to create commits, and `git push` to update the remote repository. I consider these to be the basic git commands. However, git can still be very confusing to use, and you may end up with your repository in a mess. It does get easier with practice and there is plenty of help online. You can always delete your local repository and start again from the remote version (as I have done many times before).

Now we have git installed, let's set the author information as follows:

```
git config --global user.name "Phil Jones"
git config --global user.email "pgjones@tozo.dev"
```

The highlighted values should be changed to your name and email address.

Next, we can create a repository for our code by creating a directory called *tozo* and running the following command within it:

```
git init .
```

This will create a *.git* directory that can be safely ignored. This results in the following project structure:

```
tozo
└── .git
```

As we develop, we will want git to ignore certain files and paths. We will do this by creating *.gitignore* files that list the filenames and file paths that we do not want to be part of our repository.

> **Writing good commits**
>
> The history of changes stored by git can serve as an excellent companion document for your code if git is used well. This is something that won't seem advantageous at the start, but after a year of development, it will be something you'll sorely miss if you hadn't done it from the beginning. So, I strongly recommend you write good commits.
>
> A good commit contains a single atomic change to the code. This means it is focused (doesn't combine different changes into one commit) and that it is complete (every commit leaves the code working).
>
> A good commit is also well described and reasoned. This means the commit message explains why the change has been made. This contextual information is invaluable as it will be forgotten quickly and is often required to understand the code.

With git installed, we can start committing changes; however, we should establish how we intend to combine changes, which, in my opinion, should be done by rebasing.

Rebasing rather than merging

As I put a lot of value on the git commit history, I recommend using rebases rather than merges when combining changes. The former will move local new commits on top of any remote changes, rewriting and leaving a linear clear history, whereas the latter will introduce a merge commit. To make this change, run the following code:

```
git config --global pull.rebase true
```

We've now set up our system with a package manager and version control. Next, we can install the specific tooling we need for the various aspects of the app.

Installing Python for backend development

There are a variety of languages that are suitable for backend development, and any would be a fine choice for your app. In this book, I've chosen to use Python as I find that the code is more accessible and easier to follow than other languages.

As we will be writing the backend for our app in **Python**, we will need to have it installed locally. While you may have a Python version already installed, I'd recommend you use the one installed by the system package manager, as follows:

```
brew install python
scoop install python
```

The package manager we've used so far doesn't know how to install and manage Python packages, so we also need another package manager. There are many choices in Python, and I think PDM is the best. PDM can be installed with the system package manager on Linux and macOS systems, as follows:

```
brew install pdm
```

For Windows systems, it can be installed by running the following commands:

```
scoop bucket add frostming https://github.com/frostming/scoop-
frostming.git
scoop install pdm
```

We'll keep the backend code separate in a backend folder, so please create a *backend* folder at the top level of the project with the following folder structure:

```
tozo
└── backend
    ├── src
    │   └── backend
    └── tests
```

Next, we need to inform git that there are files that we don't want to be tracked in the repository and hence it should ignore them by adding the following to *backend/.gitignore*:

```
/__pypackages__
/.mypy_cache
.pdm.toml
.pytest_cache
.venv
*.pyc
```

For PDM to manage our project, we need to run the following command in the *backend* directory:

```
pdm init
```

When prompted, you should choose the Python version installed using the system package manager earlier.

We can now focus on the specific Python tooling for fast development.

Formatting the code

Python does not have an official format or formatter; however, `black` is the de facto formatter for code and `isort` is the de facto formatter for imports. We can add both to our project by running the following command in the *backend* directory:

```
pdm add --dev black isort
```

> **The dev flag**
>
> We use the `--dev` flag here as these tools are only required for developing the backend and therefore do not need to be installed when running in production.

black and isort require the following configuration to work well together. This should be added to the end of the *backend/pyproject.toml* file (you may have to change the target-version if you are using a version of Python other than 3.10) as follows:

```
[tool.black]
target-version = ["py310"]

[tool.isort]
profile = "black"
```

The following commands will run black and isort on our code in the *src* and *tests* folders:

```
pdm run black src tests
pdm run isort src tests
```

We'll be using Jinja templates for emails sent by our app. While these templates are code, they are not Python and hence require a different formatter. Thankfully, djhtml can be used to format the templates and is added by running the following command in the *backend* folder:

```
pdm add --dev djhtml
```

The following command will run djhtml on our template code:

```
djhtml src/backend/templates --tabwidth 2 --check
```

We've now installed the tooling we need to format the code in the backend. Next, we can install the tooling we need to lint the code.

Linting the code

Python supports type hints that describe the expected types of variables, functions, and so on. We'll use type hints and tooling to check that we haven't introduced any type-related bugs. The most popular type checking tool for Python is mypy. It is installed by running the following command in the *backend* directory:

```
pdm add --dev mypy
```

The following command will run mypy over the backend code:

```
pdm run mypy src/backend/ tests/
```

With mypy helping us find type errors, we can add Flake8 to help us find other bugs. Flake8 is installed with pdm as follows:

```
pdm add --dev flake8
```

Flake8 must be configured to work with black and mypy by adding the following to *backend/ setup.cfg*:

```
[flake8]
max-line-length = 88
extend-ignore = E203
```

Flake8 is used by running the following command:

```
pdm run flake8 src/ tests/
```

There is another type of bug that we can use tooling to help us find, and these are related to security. A good example would be checking for a SQL injection vulnerability. Bandit is another linter that helps identify these bugs, and it is installed by running the following command in the *backend* directory:

```
pdm add --dev bandit
```

Bandit only needs to lint the src code as the test code does not run during production. To run Bandit over the src code, the following command is used:

```
pdm run bandit -r src/
```

> **Bandit ModuleNotFoundErrors**
>
> Bandit may fail to run with the error ModuleNotFoundError: No module named 'pkg_resources'. If this happens, then run pdm add --dev setuptools to add the missing module.

We now have tooling looking for bugs, but we can also add tooling to look for unused code. This is helpful as code can often be forgotten during refactoring, leaving files that are much more complex to read and understand than they should be. I like to use vulture to find unused code, and it is installed by running the following command in the *backend* directory:

```
pdm add --dev vulture
```

Unfortunately, `vulture` can report false positives, so I like to configure it to be 100% confident when reporting issues by adding the following configuration to *backend/pyproject.toml*:

```
[tool.vulture]
min_confidence = 100
```

Like Bandit, it is best to run `vulture` over the `src` code only (not the tests) via the following command:

```
pdm run vulture src/
```

Now, let's look at what we need to test the code.

Testing the code

Python has `unittest` as part of its standard library, however, I think using `pytest` is superior. `pytest` is very feature-rich and allows for very simple and clear tests, such as the following small example that tests that a simple addition is correct:

```
def test_addition():
    assert 1 + 1 == 2
```

`pytest` requires the `pytest-asyncio` plugin to test async code, and they are both installed with pdm as follows:

```
pdm add --dev pytest pytest-asyncio
```

`pytest` is best configured to show local variables on test failure as this makes it much easier to understand why the test is failing. In addition, the `asyncio` mode should be set to `auto` to make writing async tests easier. The following configuration should be placed in *backend/pyproject.toml*:

```
[tool.pytest.ini_options]
addopts = "--showlocals"
asyncio_mode = "auto"
pythonpath = ["src"]
```

To run the tests, `pytest` is invoked with the `tests` path as follows:

```
pdm run pytest tests
```

Now that we've installed all of the tooling, we need some simple commands to run it.

Scripting the commands

We've added a lot of useful tooling to our project; however, each one had a different unique command that we'd have to remember. This is something we can simplify by making use of PDM's scripting feature as it can be used to map PDM commands to the required commands. We will add the following three PDM scripting commands:

- `pdm run format` to run the formatting tooling and format the code
- `pdm run lint` to run the linting tooling and lint the code
- `pdm run test` to run the tests

PDM's scripting requires these script commands to be added to the *backend/pyproject.toml* file as follows:

```
[tool.pdm.scripts]
format-black = "black src/ tests/"
format-djhtml = "djhtml src/backend/templates -t 2 --in-place"
format-isort = "isort src tests"
format = {composite = ["format-black", "format-djhtml",
"format-isort"]}
lint-bandit = "bandit -r src/"
lint-black = "black --check --diff src/ tests/"
lint-djhtml = "djhtml src/backend/templates -t 2 --check"
lint-flake8 = "flake8 src/ tests/"
lint-isort = "isort --check --diff src tests"
lint-mypy = "mypy src/backend tests"
lint-vulture = "vulture src"
lint = {composite = ["lint-bandit", "lint-black", "lint-
djhtml", "lint-flake8", "lint-isort", "lint-mypy", "lint-
vulture"]}
test = "pytest tests/"
```

With the backend tooling in place and accessible via easy-to-remember commands, we can now do the same for the frontend.

Installing NodeJS for frontend development

As we want our app to run in the browser, we will need to write the frontend in JavaScript or a language that compiles to it. There are many good choices, but I've chosen to use **TypeScript** as it is JavaScript with the addition of typing (as in, it is the same basic language). This means it is close to the required runtime language and has the additional safety and documentation from the typing.

As we will be writing the frontend in TypeScript, we will need **NodeJS** installed to compile TypeScript to the JavaScript that will run in the browser. NodeJS is best installed with the system package manager as follows:

```
brew install node
scoop install nodejs
```

Unlike Python, where we installed a specific package manager, NodeJS comes with one called npm. We'll use npm to manage the frontend dependencies and tooling. npm also includes the npx tool that we will use to run one-off scripts.

As with the backend, we'll separate the frontend code into a frontend folder. Then, we'll use the create-react-app tool in this new folder to set everything up by running the following command in the project directory:

```
npx create-react-app frontend --template typescript
```

It should give the following folder structure:

```
tozo
└── frontend
    ├── node_modules
    ├── public
    └── src
```

Of the files also installed, only the *frontend/package.json, frontend/package-lock.json, frontend/tsconfig.json, frontend/.gitignore, frontend/src/react-app-env.d.ts*, and *frontend/public/index.html* files matter at the moment, so you can delete or adapt the other files as you'd like.

We can now focus on the specific NodeJS tooling for fast development.

Formatting the code

TypeScript does not have an official format/formatter; however, Prettier is the de facto formatter. We should add it to the project as a development dependency by running the following command in the *frontend* directory:

```
npm install --save-dev prettier
```

> **The --save-dev flag**
>
> We use the --save-dev flag here as these tools are only required to develop the frontend, and therefore do not need to be installed when running in production.

By default, Prettier does not add trailing commas, which is different from the style used in Python. To be consistent and therefore not have to think about this, Prettier can be configured by adding the following section to *frontend/package.json*:

```
"prettier": {
  "trailingComma": "all"
}
```

The following command will then run Prettier over our code:

```
npx prettier --parser typescript --write "src/**/*.{ts,tsx}"
```

We've now installed the tooling to format the code and we can focus on the tooling to lint it.

Linting the code

In the preceding section, we required a linter to type check our Python code, however, as we are using TypeScript, we do not need to install anything extra to type check. However, we can install linters to check for other bugs; the de facto linter for TypeScript and JavaScript is `eslint`, which is installed by running the following command in the *frontend* directory:

```
npm install --save-dev eslint
```

By default, `eslint` is not compatible with Prettier; fortunately, the `eslint-config-prettier` package configures `eslint` to be compatible. It is installed by running the following command in the *frontend* directory:

```
npm install --save-dev eslint-config-prettier
```

As with the backend, we should order our imports using `eslint-plugin-import`, which is installed with npm as follows:

```
npm install --save-dev eslint-plugin-import
```

These linters are then configured by replacing the existing `eslintConfig` section with the following in *frontend/package.json*:

```
"eslintConfig": {
  "extends": [
    "react-app",
    "react-app/jest",
    "plugin:import/errors",
    "plugin:import/warnings",
```

```
        "plugin:import/typescript",
        "prettier"
    ]
}
```

The highlighted lines will already be present.

`eslint` can be run over our code via the following command:

```
npx eslint "src/**/*.{ts,tsx}"
```

`eslint` can also fix some of the issues it identifies via the use of the `--fix` flag as follows:

```
npx eslint --fix "src/**/*.{ts,tsx}"
```

We've now installed the tooling to lint the code and we can focus on the tooling to test it.

Testing the code

The `create-react-app` tool used earlier also installed a test runner called Jest, which we can invoke by running the following:

```
npm run test
```

Jest allows for tests to be written using an `expect` syntax, as shown in the following example:

```
test('addition', () => {
    expect(1 + 1).toBe(2);
});
```

With the testing tooling present, we can focus on analyzing the built bundle.

Analyzing the bundle

The frontend code will be delivered as bundles (in chunks) to the user. These bundles, especially the main bundle, should be small so that the user isn't waiting too long for the code to be downloaded. To check the bundle size and analyze what is included in each bundle, I use `source-map-explorer`, which is installed by running the following command in the *frontend* directory:

```
npm install --save-dev source-map-explorer
```

Before we can analyze the bundle sizes, we first need to build them by running the following command:

```
npm run build
```

Then, we can analyze them via this command:

```
npx source-map-explorer build/static/js/*.js
```

The output from the preceding command is shown in *Figure 1.2*:

Bundle: [combined] (145.03 KB) ⌄

```
/ · 145.03 KB · 100.0%
main.2106ee1a.js · 140.54 KB · 96.9%
.. · 139.75 KB · 96.4%
node_modules · 137.51 KB · 94.8%        W
                                        ·
                                        2
                                        K
                                        ·
```

Figure 1.2: The output from source-map-explorer showing that the main bundle is 141 KB

Each bundle should be as small as possible, with a good rule of thumb being that bundles should be split when the bundle exceeds 1 MB. We'll find that we need to do this when we add a password complexity analyzer to the frontend in *Chapter 4, Creating a Reusable Frontend with React*.

Scripting the commands

To match the backend, we want to add the following commands:

- `npm run analyze` to run the bundle analyzer
- `npm run format` to run the formatting tooling and format the code
- `npm run lint` to run the linting tooling
- `npm run test` to run the tests

As `npm run test` is already present, we only need to add the other three. This is done by adding the following to the `scripts` section in *frontend/package.json*:

```
"scripts": {
  "analyze": "npm run build && source-map-explorer \"build/
static/js/*.js\"",
  "format": "eslint --fix \"src/**/*.{ts,tsx}\" && prettier
--parser typescript --write \"src/**/*.{ts,tsx}\"",
  "lint": " eslint \"src/**/*.{ts,tsx}\" && prettier --parser
typescript --list-different  \"src/**/*.{ts,tsx}\"",
  "start": "react-scripts start",
```

```
    "build": "react-scripts build",
    "test": "react-scripts test",
    "eject": "react-scripts eject"
}
```

The highlighted lines will already be present in the section.

With the frontend tooling in place and accessible via the easy-to-remember commands, we can now do the same for the infrastructure.

Installing Terraform for infrastructure development

We'll need to create and manage remote infrastructure, starting with a remote repository that we will use to develop the app with other developers or to simply backup our code. This remote infrastructure could be created manually, for example, using GitHub's web interface. However, by using an Infrastructure as a Code tool, we can record all of the changes we make, and then if anything goes wrong, we can rerun our code and restore everything to a known state.

I find **Terraform** to be the best tool to manage infrastructure, which we can install as follows:

```
brew install terraform
scoop install terraform
```

With Terraform installed, we can create a folder within our repository for the infrastructure code as follows:

```
mkdir infrastructure
```

Our repository should now have the following structure:

```
tozo
├── backend
├── frontend
└── infrastructure
```

As with the backend and frontend, we'll need to install tooling to help development. In addition, for the infrastructure, we'll need tooling to manage secrets.

Managing secrets

To allow Terraform to manage our infrastructure, we will need to provide passwords, keys, and other secrets. These secrets will need to be stored (and used) in a secure fashion – simply storing passwords in plain text in the repository is a common way to be hacked. We will instead encrypt the secrets and store the encrypted file in the repository. This means we'll have to keep the encryption key secret, which I recommend you do by using a password manager such as BitWarden.

To encrypt the secrets, we can use `ansible-vault`, which is installed using the Python package manager, `pip`, as follows:

```
pip install ansible-vault
```

> **pip or PDM**
>
> pip is a tool for installing packages, whereas PDM is a project management tool. As we don't have an infrastructure project to manage, it makes more sense to use pip to install `ansible-vault`. However, this is the only time we'll directly use pip.

To configure `ansible-vault`, we need to provide the encryption key. To do so, add your encryption key to *infrastructure/.ansible-vault* and inform Ansible that it is stored there by adding the following to *infrastructure/ansible.cfg*:

```
[defaults]
vault_password_file = .ansible-vault
```

We'll need to encrypt two files: Terraform's state, `terraform.tfstate`, and our collection of secret variables, `secrets.auto.tfvars`. The commands to do so are the following:

```
ansible-vault encrypt secrets.auto.tfvars --output=secrets.
auto.tfvars.vault
ansible-vault encrypt terraform.tfstate --output=terraform.
tfstate.vault
```

We will also need to decrypt these files, which is done via the following commands:

```
ansible-vault decrypt secrets.auto.tfvars.vault
--output=secrets.auto.tfvars
ansible-vault decrypt terraform.tfstate.vault
--output=terraform.tfstate
```

To ensure that the password file, encrypted files, and general Terraform autogenerated files aren't considered part of the repository, the following should be added to *infrastructure/.gitignore*:

```
.ansible-vault
secrets.auto.tfvars
terraform.tfstate
*.backup
.terraform.lock.hcl
.terraform/
```

Terraform is now set up and ready to use, which means we can focus on the development tooling.

Formatting, linting, and testing the code

Terraform comes with a built-in formatter, which is invoked via the following command:

```
terraform fmt
```

This formatter also supports a check mode to use when linting, as follows:

```
terraform fmt --check=true
```

Terraform also comes with a tool to lint your code, as follows:

```
terraform validate
```

Testing Terraform code is harder as almost all of the code depends on an interaction with a third-party service. Instead, I find running and checking that the output makes sense to be the only way to test what the code will do. Terraform will provide an output of what it plans to do by running the following command:

```
terraform plan
```

This is all we need to install and set up to manage all of the infrastructure we'll install in this book. We can now focus on the database.

Installing PostgreSQL for database development

Our app will need to store data (the to-dos) in a structured form, which makes a database an ideal choice. This database will need to be running locally to allow us to develop with it, so we need to install it. The database I prefer is **PostgreSQL**, which is a SQL-based relational database. I prefer it as it is very widely supported, and very powerful.

PostgreSQL is installed using the system package manager as follows:

```
brew install postgres
scoop install postgresql
```

If using `brew`, you will likely need to start `postgresql` as a service that runs in the background, as follows:

```
brew services start postgresql
```

In addition, when using `brew`, we need to create a superuser, which by convention is called *postgres*. This user is created with the following command:

```
createuser -s postgres
```

However, with `scoop`, you will have to start the PostgreSQL database whenever you wish to use it with the following command:

```
pg_ctl start
```

With the addition of the database tooling, we have all of the local tooling we need to develop our app. This means we can focus on the remote tooling, a GitHub repository.

Adopting a collaborative development process using GitHub

While you may be working on your own, it is good practice to adopt a development process that allows others to collaborate and one that ensures that the code is always ready to be deployed to production. We will achieve both aims by using a remote repository and **Continuous Integration** (**CI**).

A remote repository acts as a backup for all your code and makes it much easier to set up CI (testing, linting, and so on). We'll use GitHub as I find it to have all the features needed, although other platforms, such as GitLab, are also valid and commonly used in the industry.

Rather than creating the repository through GitHub's UI, we'll use Terraform as set up earlier. To do so, we'll first need a personal access token from GitHub, as explained at `https://docs.github.com/en/authentication/keeping-your-account-and-data-secure/creating-a-personal-access-token`. The token will need the `repo`, `workflow`, and `delete_repo` scopes. This token is a secret and hence best placed in *infrastructure/secrets.auto.tfvars* and encrypted as described earlier in the *Managing secrets* section. The code should be placed into *infrastructure/secrets.auto.tfvars* as follows (replace `abc1234` with your token):

```
github_token = "abc1234"
```

Terraform itself does not know how to interact with GitHub, which means that we need to install the GitHub provider to do so. This is done by adding the following code to *infrastructure/main.tf*:

```
terraform {
  required_providers {
    github = {
      source  = "integrations/github"
      version = "~> 4.0"
    }
  }
  required_version = ">=1.0"
}
```

With the provider present, we can describe the repository we would like to exist by adding the following code to *infrastructure/github.tf*:

```
variable "github_token" {
  sensitive = true
}

provider "github" {
  token = var.github_token
}

resource "github_repository" "tozo" {
  name       = "tozo"
  visibility = "private"
}
```

Finally, to actually create the repository, we need to initialize and apply Terraform as follows:

```
terraform init
terraform apply
```

We should now set up `git` so that it knows about the remote repository. To do this, we'll need the correct path, which will depend on your GitHub account name and the name of your project. As my GitHub account name is *pgjones* and this project is called *tozo*, the path is *pgjones/tozo*, making the following command:

```
git remote add origin git@github.com:pgjones/tozo.git
```

To have our local branch track the remote `origin main` branch, run the following command:

```
git push --set-upstream origin main
```

To push our local changes on our `main` branch to the remote `feature` branch, run the following command:

```
git push origin main:feature
```

To pull the remote `main` branch to update our local branch, run the following command:

```
git pull origin main
```

Most in this industry operate a development workflow based on merge (pull) requests, which we'll also adopt. This workflow consists of the following steps:

1. Develop a feature locally consisting of as few commits as makes sense (small changes).
2. Push the feature to a remote `feature` branch.
3. Open a merge request based on that branch.
4. Review the merge request, merging it to the `main` branch only if CI passes.
5. Pull the latest `main` branch and repeat.

With the repository created, we can now look at adding CI.

Adding continuous integration

GitHub provides a CI system called Actions that has a free tier, which we'll use. To start, we need to create the following folder structure:

```
tozo
└── .github
    └── workflows
```

Now we can configure a workflow that runs jobs on every change to the main branch and every merge request by adding the following code to *.github/workflows/ci.yml*:

```
name: CI

on:
  push:
    branches: [ main ]
  pull_request:
    branches: [ main ]
  workflow_dispatch:

jobs:
```

This allows us to add jobs for the infrastructure, backend, and frontend.

Adding CI for the infrastructure code

We previously set up the commands to format and lint the infrastructure code as follows:

```
terraform fmt --check=true
terraform validate
```

To have these run as part of CI, we need to add the following job to the *.github/workflows/ci.yml* file within the jobs section:

```
  infrastructure:
    runs-on: ubuntu-latest

    steps:
      - name: Install Terraform
        run: |
          sudo apt-get update && sudo apt-get install -y gnupg
            software-properties-common curl
          curl -fsSL https://apt.releases.hashicorp.com/gpg |
            sudo apt-key add -
          sudo apt-add-repository "deb [arch=amd64] https://
            apt.releases.hashicorp.com $(lsb_release -cs) main"
          sudo apt-get update && sudo apt-get install terraform
```

```
- uses: actions/checkout@v3

- name: Initialise Terraform
  run: terraform init

- name: Check the formatting
  run: terraform fmt --check=true --recursive

- name: Validate the code
  run: terraform validate
```

We can now add a job for the backend code.

Adding CI for the backend code

We previously set up the commands to format, lint, and test the backend code as follows:

```
pdm run format
pdm run lint
pdm run test
```

To have these run as part of CI, we will need to have a database service running as well, as the tests run against the database. Fortunately, GitHub supports PostgreSQL database services by running a PostgreSQL database alongside the CI job. We can make use of this database service and run the commands by adding the following job to the jobs section in *.github/workflows/ci.yml*:

```
backend:
  runs-on: ubuntu-latest

  container: python:3.10.1-slim-bullseye

  services:
    postgres:
      image: postgres
      env:
        POSTGRES_DB: tozo_test
        POSTGRES_USER: tozo
        POSTGRES_PASSWORD: tozo
        POSTGRES_HOST_AUTH_METHOD: "trust"
```

```
        options: >-
          --health-cmd pg_isready
          --health-interval 10s
          --health-timeout 5s
          --health-retries 5

  defaults:
    run:
      working-directory: backend

  env:
    TOZO_QUART_DB_DATABASE_URL: "postgresql://tozo:tozo@
      postgres:5432/tozo_test"

  steps:
    - uses: actions/checkout@v3

    - name: Install system dependencies
      run: apt-get update && apt-get install -y postgresql
        postgresql-contrib

    - name: Initialise dependencies
      run: |
        pip install pdm
        pdm install

    - name: Linting
      run: pdm run lint

    - name: Testing
      run: pdm run test
```

We can now add a job for the frontend code.

Adding CI for the frontend code

We previously set up the commands to format, lint, test, and build the frontend code as follows:

```
npm run format
npm run lint
npm run test
npm run build
```

We can make use of the service and run the commands by adding the following job to the jobs section of *.github/workflows/ci.yml*:

```
frontend:
  runs-on: ubuntu-latest

  defaults:
    run:
      working-directory: frontend

  steps:
    - name: Use Node.js
      uses: actions/setup-node@v2
      with:
        node-version: '18'

    - uses: actions/checkout@v3

    - name: Initialise dependencies
      run: npm ci --cache .npm --prefer-offline

    - name: Check formatting
      run: npm run format

    - name: Linting
      run: npm run lint

    - name: Testing
      run: npm run test
```

```
    - name: Build
      run: npm run build
```

We now have everything we need in place to start developing our app. The folder structure at this stage is as follows:

```
tozo
├── .github
│   └── workflows
├── backend
│   ├── src
│   │   └── backend
│   └── tests
├── frontend
│   ├── public
│   └── src
└── infrastructure
```

We now have all of our checks running on every change to the `main` branch and for every pull request. This should ensure that our code remains at a high quality and alert us to any issues that may otherwise be missed.

Summary

In this chapter, we set up all of the tooling we need to develop our app. We started by installing a system package manager, which we then used to install and set up git. With git, we created our local repository and started to commit code. We installed Python, NodeJS, Terraform, and the tooling required to format, lint, and test the code. Finally, we used Terraform to create and set up a remote GitHub repository with working CI, ensuring that our code is automatically checked on every change.

The tooling we've installed in this chapter is required to develop the app described in the following chapters. It will also allow you to do so quickly, as the tooling will help you quickly identify issues and errors with the code.

In the next chapter, we'll start developing the backend of our app, with the focus being on setting up the app framework and extensions that support the features we want, for example, authentication.

Further reading

It is often useful to switch versions of Python and NodeJS to test the app before upgrading it. To do this, I'd recommend pyenv (`https://github.com/pyenv/pyenv`) and n (`https://github.com/tj/n`) for Python and NodeJS, respectively.

Part 2
Building a To-Do
App

Now, we will build a fully functional to-do tracking application using Quart and React. The app will include many common features, such as authentication, user management, styled pages, and forms.

This part consists of the following chapters:

2

Creating a Reusable Backend with Quart

In the preceding chapter, we installed the tooling we need to develop our app, which means we can start building the backend. The backend runs on the server as opposed to the frontend, which runs in the client's web browser. In our setup, the backend will need to be the interface between the database and the frontend, providing an API to access and edit the to-dos (see *Figure 2.1*):

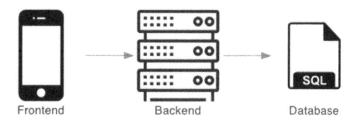

Figure 2.1: A schematic overview of the desired setup

Alongside providing an API, the backend will also need to connect to the database, manage user sessions, protect itself against heavy and incorrect usage, and send emails to users. In this chapter, we will build a backend with these features. At the end of the chapter, we will have built a reusable backend that any API can be built with. Alternatively, the features can be taken in parts to add to your own app.

So, in this chapter, we will cover the following topics:

- Creating a basic Quart app
- Including user accounts
- Protecting the app
- Connecting to the database
- Sending emails

Technical requirements

The following additional folders are required in this chapter and should be created:

```
tozo
└── backend
    ├── src
    │   └── backend
    │       ├── blueprints
    │       ├── lib
    │       └── templates
    └── tests
        ├── blueprints
        └── lib
```

Empty *backend/src/backend/__init__.py*, *backend/src/backend/blueprints/__init__.py*, *backend/src/backend/lib/__init__.py*, *backend/tests/__init__.py*, *backend/tests/blueprints/__init__.py*, and *backend/tests/lib/__init__.py* files should be created.

To follow the development in this chapter, use the companion repository at `https://github.com/pgjones/tozo` and see the commits between the tags `r1-ch2-start` and `r1-ch2-end`.

Creating a basic Quart app

To begin, we can make a basic API that responds to requests with a simple response. This is something I like to term a ping-pong route as the request is the ping and the response is the pong. To do this, I've chosen to use the Quart framework. **Quart** is a web microframework with an ecosystem of extensions that we will use to add additional functionality.

> **Using Flask as an alternative**
>
> Quart is the async version of the very popular Flask framework, which allows us to use modern async libraries. However, if you are already familiar with Flask, you can adapt the code in this book without too much difficulty; see `https://quart.palletsprojects.com/en/latest/how_to_guides/flask_migration.html` for more information.

To use Quart, we must first add it with pdm by running the following command in the *backend* directory:

```
pdm add quart
```

We can now create a Quart app by adding the following code to *backend/src/backend/run.py*:

```
from quart import Quart


app = Quart(__name__)
```

This allows us to add functions, called route handlers, which are called when a request matches the given HTTP method and path and returns the response. For our basic app, we want requests to *GET /control/ping/* to be responded to. This is achieved by adding the following code to *backend/src/backend/run.py*:

```
from quart import ResponseReturnValue


@app.get("/control/ping/")
async def ping() -> ResponseReturnValue:
    return {"ping": "pong"}
```

Now that there is code to create the app with a ping route, we should set up the tooling so that the server starts locally and serves requests. As with the backend tooling, we need to add a new script name to *backend/pyproject.toml* as follows:

```
[tool.pdm.scripts]
start = "quart --app src/backend/run.py run --port 5050"
```

The preceding code allows the following command to start the backend app when it is run in the *backend* directory, as follows:

```
pdm run start
```

With this command running, we can check whether the ping route works by running the following command in any directory:

```
curl localhost:5050/control/ping/
```

Alternatively, you could enter http://localhost:5050/control/ping/ in your browser, as shown in *Figure 2.2*:

Figure 2.2: The control ping route when visited in the browser

---

Using curl

`curl` (`https://curl.se/docs/manpage.html`) is an excellent command-line tool to make HTTP requests. `curl` is installed on most systems by default, but if you find that you don't have it, you can use the system package manager to install it (`brew install curl` or `scoop install curl`).

Without any options, `curl` makes a GET request, and you can switch to a POST request using the `-X POST` option, or you can send JSON data using the `--json '{"tool":` `"curl"}'` option.

This is all that is required for a basic backend; however, we need more functionality and more certainty that the code works. We'll achieve this by adding testing, using blueprints, adding configuration, and ensuring a consistent JSON error response.

Testing the ping route

It is good practice to test whether the route works as expected. To do this, we can add the following test to *backend/tests/test_run.py*:

```
from backend.run import app
```

```
async def test_control() -> None:
    test_client = app.test_client()
    response = await test_client.get("/control/ping/")
    assert (await response.get_json())["ping"] == "pong"
```

With the test code in place, we can run pdm run test and see whether it both runs and passes.

> **Warning about a common await error**
>
> I've found it common to incorrectly await the wrong thing in Python, and it seems common with others as well. The issue is often seen with code such as:
>
> ```
> await response.get_json()["ping"].
> ```
>
> This will fail with the coroutine cannot be indexed error, as the coroutine returned by response.get_json() must be awaited before it is indexed. This issue is fixed by adding parenthesis in the right place, which in this case is as follows:
>
> ```
> (await response.get_json())["ping"].
> ```

Now that we have a working ping-pong route, we need to consider how to add many more routes, which, for clarity, is best done using blueprints.

Using blueprints for clearer code

We added the ping route handler to the same file as the app (*backend/src/backend/run.py*) as it is the easiest way to start; however, as we add more route handlers, the file will quickly become unclear and difficult to update. Quart provides blueprints to help structure code as the app gets bigger. As we will be adding more route handlers, we'll convert what we have so far into blueprints.

We can now move the ping route handler to a control blueprint by adding the following code to *backend/src/backend/blueprints/control.py*:

```
from quart import Blueprint, ResponseReturnValue

blueprint = Blueprint("control", __name__)

@blueprint.get("/control/ping/")
async def ping() -> ResponseReturnValue:
    return {"ping": "pong"}
```

We can then register it with the app by changing *backend/src/backend/run.py* to the following:

```
from quart import Quart


from backend.blueprints.control import blueprint as control_
blueprint


app = Quart(__name__)


app.register_blueprint(control_blueprint)
```

The existing tests will continue to work; however, I think the location of the test should shadow the location of the code it is testing. This makes it easier to understand where the tests are, and what the tests should be testing. Therefore, we need to move *backend/tests/test_run.py* to *backend/tests/blueprints/test_control.py*.

You should now have the following backend files and structure:

```
tozo
└── backend
    ├── pdm.lock
    ├── pyproject.toml
    ├── setup.cfg
    ├── src
    │   └── backend
    │       ├── blueprints
    │       │   ├── __init__.py
    │       │   └── control.py
    │       ├── __init__.py
    │       └── run.py
    └── tests
        ├── blueprints
        │   ├── __init__.py
        │   └── test_control.py
        └── __init__.py
```

We'll use a blueprint for each logical collection of features in our app and follow this structure throughout. We can now focus on configuring the app to run in the various environments we will use.

Configuring the app

We need to run our app in multiple environments, notably development, testing, CI, and production. To do so, we'll need to change some settings in each; for example, the database connection. Configuration allows us to change these settings without having to alter the code. It also allows secrets to be managed separately from the code, and hence more securely.

I find environment variables to be the best way to provide configuration, with each environment having different values for the same variable. We can instruct Quart to load the configuration from prefixed environment variables. The prefix ensures that only relevant environment variables are considered; by default, the prefix is QUART_, but we'll change it to TOZO_. To do so, we'll need to add the following change to *backend/src/backend/run.py* so that the config is loaded immediately after the app is created:

```
app = Quart(__name__)
app.config.from_prefixed_env(prefix="TOZO")
```

The highlighted line of code should already be present.

In production, we'll define the environment variables using a Terraform script, whereas locally, we will load environment variables from a file. First, for development, we need to add the following to *backend/development.env*:

```
TOZO_BASE_URL="localhost:5050"
TOZO_DEBUG=true
TOZO_SECRET_KEY="secret key"
```

Second, for testing, we need to add the following to *backend/testing.env*:

```
TOZO_BASE_URL="localhost:5050"
TOZO_DEBUG=true
TOZO_SECRET_KEY="secret key"
TOZO_TESTING=true
```

Now that the files exist, we can adapt the PDM scripts to load them when starting the app or running tests by making the following change to *backend/pyproject.toml*:

```
[tool.pdm.scripts]
start = {cmd = "quart --app src/backend/run.py run --port
  5050", env_file = "development.env"}
test = {cmd = "pytest tests/", env_file = "testing.env"}
```

These small modifications to the scripts will ensure that the environment is automatically loaded when using the `pdm run start` and `pdm run test` commands. We'll now look at an often-overlooked feature, which is consistent error responses.

Ensuring error responses are JSON

As we are writing a backend API that serves JSON, it is important that all responses use JSON, including error responses. Therefore, rather than using the Quart built-in error responses, we will use our own that explicitly result in a JSON response.

Error responses are usually signified by a status code in the 400-500 range. However, the status code alone cannot always convey enough information. For example, when registering a new member, a status code of 400 is expected for a request with an invalid email address and a request with a weak password. Hence, there is a need to return an additional code to separate these cases. We can do so by adding the following code to *backend/src/backend/lib/api_error.py*:

```
class APIError(Exception):
    def __init__(self, status_code: int, code: str) -> None:
        self.status_code = status_code
        self.code = code
```

With `APIError` available, we can now inform Quart how to handle it by adding the following code to *backend/src/backend/run.py*:

```
from quart import ResponseReturnValue

from backend.lib.api_error import APIError

@app.errorhandler(APIError)  # type: ignore
async def handle_api_error(error: APIError) ->
ResponseReturnValue:
    return {"code": error.code}, error.status_code
```

We should also inform Quart how to handle any other unexpected errors, such as those that would result in a 500 "Internal Server Error" response, as follows:

```
@app.errorhandler(500)
async def handle_generic_error(
    error: Exception
) -> ResponseReturnValue:
    return {"code": "INTERNAL_SERVER_ERROR"}, 500
```

We now have a basic Quart app setup to allow us to add all of the features we need for our actual app, starting with the ability to manage user accounts.

Including user accounts

As we want users to be able to log into our app, we will need to **authenticate** that the client is who they claim to be. Thereafter, we need to ensure that each user only gets to see their own to-dos. This is typically achieved by the user entering a username and password, which are then checked against stored versions.

We will need to authenticate every request the user makes to the backend; however, we ideally only want the user to enter their username and password once (until they log out). We can achieve this by saving information to a cookie when the user logs in, as the browser will then send us the cookie with every request.

We will need to save a piece of identifying information to the cookie when the user logs in and starts the session; for example, their user ID. We can then read the cookie on every request and identify which user it is. However, cookies can be edited, or faked, by the client so we need to ensure that the information in the cookie hasn't been tampered with.

We can prevent tampering by signing the information in the cookie. Signing is where a cryptographic function is applied to the data using a secret key to create a signature. This signature is then stored with the data, allowing the stored signature to be checked against a recalculated version.

Quart-Auth is a Quart extension that does this for us by managing cookies and the data stored in them. Quart-Auth is installed by running the following command in the *backend* directory:

```
pdm add quart-auth
```

Then, you need to activate `AuthManager` when creating the app in *backend/src/backend/run.py*, as follows:

```
from quart_auth import AuthManager


auth_manager = AuthManager(app)
```

While Quart-Auth comes with a sensible set of defaults for securing the cookie, our usage allows us to be more secure. Specifically, we can utilize the Strict SameSite setting, rather than the Lax setting that Quart-Auth defaults to. This is because we only need to authenticate non-navigation requests to the API routes.

> **SameSite**
>
> The SameSite setting ensures that cookie data is only sent with requests that originate from the given domain. This prevents other websites from initiating requests with the cookie data. To find out more information about SameSite, you can follow this link: `https://developer.mozilla.org/en-US/docs/Web/HTTP/Headers/Set-Cookie/SameSite`.

To add the Strict SameSite setting, add the following to *backend/development.env* and *backend/testing.env*:

```
TOZO_QUART_AUTH_COOKIE_SAMESITE="Strict"
```

However, we will need to disable the secure cookie flag in development as we aren't using HTTPS. This is done by adding the following to *backend/development.env* and *backend/testing.env*:

```
TOZO_QUART_AUTH_COOKIE_SECURE=false
```

With Quart-Auth managing the session, we now need to store the passwords, ensure that they are strong, and allow for passwordless authentication.

Securely storing passwords

While we can now manage a user's session, in order to start it, the user needs to log in by providing an email and password. While the emails are fine to store directly in the database, extra care must be taken with the passwords. This is because users often use the same password across many websites/services, and if it were to leak from our app, we could have potentially leaked access to many other websites as well. Therefore, instead of storing the password directly, we will hash the password and store that.

A **password hash** is the result of applying a hashing operation to the plain-text password. A good hashing operation should ensure that the resultant hash cannot be turned back into the plain-text password and that each distinct plain-text password produces a different hash result.

I like to use `bcrypt` as the hashing operation as it meets both of these requirements and is easy to use. `bcrypt` is installed by running the following command in the *backend* directory:

```
pdm add bcrypt
```

With `bcrypt` installed, we can hash passwords with generated salt per password as follows:

```
import bcrypt

hashed = bcrypt.hashpw(password, bcrypt.gensalt(rounds=14))
```

Checking whether a supplied password matches the hashed password is then done via the following code:

```
match = bcrypt.checkpw(password, hashed)
```

We will use `bcrypt` in the login and registration functionality we'll add in *Chapter 3, Building the API*. Next, we need to check whether the passwords are strong enough.

> **Salting the password**
>
> When hashing passwords, it is best practice to **salt** them as well. This means that an additional string (`salt`) is added to the password before the hash is calculated. As the salt is meant to be different for every stored password, it ensures that the same password hashed in two different implementations has a different hash. Hence, adding salt is an additional security measure that we do via the `bcrypt.gensalt` function.

Ensuring passwords are strong

Users often choose weak passwords, which leave their account vulnerable. To protect against this, we should ensure that our users choose strong passwords. To do this, I like to use `zxcvbn` as it gives a score indicating the strength of the password. It is installed by running the following command in the *backend* directory:

```
pdm add zxcvbn
```

It is then used to give a score, as follows:

```
from zxcvbn import zxcvbn

score = zxcvbn(password).score
```

The score is a value between 0 and 4, of which I usually consider scores of 3 or 4 good. Therefore, we will prevent passwords with lower scores from being used.

We will make use of `zxcvbn` when adding registration and change password functionality in the following chapter. Next, we need to consider how the user authenticates without a password; for example, when they have forgotten it.

Allowing password-less authentication

There are a few circumstances where users are unable to provide a password but can prove that they have access to the account's email address. A prime example of this is when a user forgets their password and wishes to reset it. In these situations, we need to email the user a token that they can provide back to us, thereby authenticating them as the user in charge of the email. For this to work, the token must identify the user, and malicious users must not be able to tamper with the token or create their own tokens.

To create a token, we can sign the user's ID using a cryptographic **hash function**, secret key, and salt.

This will ensure that a malicious user cannot alter the token without generating a correct signature, which requires our secret key. To do this, we can use `itsdangerous`, which is also what Quart-Auth uses for the cookies. `itsdangerous` is installed by running the following command in the *backend* directory:

```
pdm add itsdangerous
```

As this approach does not encrypt the signed data, it is important to remember that users will be able to read anything we place in the token. Therefore, we must not put anything sensitive in the token (the user ID is not sensitive).

We will also add a timestamp to our tokens; this way we can ensure that they expire after a specific period of time. In addition, as we want to be able to use the token in links, we need to use the `URLSafeTimedSerializer`. We can create a token with the user's ID as follows:

```
from itsdangerous import URLSafeTimedSerializer
from quart import current_app

serializer = URLSafeTimedSerializer(
    current_app.secret_key, salt="salt"
)
token = serializer.dumps(user_id)
```

The token can then be read and checked as follows:

```
from itsdangerous import BadSignature, SignatureExpired

from backend.lib.api_error import APIError

signer = URLSafeTimedSerializer(
    current_app.secret_key, salt="salt"
)
try:
    user_id = signer.loads(token, max_age=ONE_DAY)
except (SignatureExpired):
    raise APIError(403, "TOKEN_EXPIRED")
except (BadSignature):
    raise APIError(400, "TOKEN_INVALID")
else:
    # Use the user_id safely
```

As we are using timed tokens, we will need to control time when we are testing. For example, if we want to test an expired token, we will need to create the token at a time whereby it will be expired when checked. To do this, we can use `freezegun`, which is installed by running the following command in the *backend* directory:

```
pdm add --dev freezegun
```

Then, we can use the following code in our tests to create an old token:

```
from freezegun import freeze_time

with freeze_time("2020-01-01"):
    signer = URLSafeTimedSerializer(
        app.secret_key, salt="salt"
    )
    token = signer.dumps(1)
```

This token can then be used to test how a route handler responds to a token that is out of date.

We will use `itsdangerous` and `freezegun` in the forgotten password functionality we'll add in the following chapter.

Next, as there are malicious users that will attempt to attack our app, we'll need to protect it.

Protecting the app

Shortly after you deploy your app in production, users will at best, misuse it, and at worst, attack it. It is therefore worthwhile being defensive from the outset by adding rate limiting and request validation.

Rate limiting limits the rate at which a remote client can make requests to the app. This prevents a user from overloading the app with their requests, thereby preventing other users from using the app.

Validation ensures that the JSON data received (or replied) matches an expected structure. This is helpful as it means an error message is displayed if the JSON data is structurally incorrect. It also mitigates against users sending structures that result in errors or issues in the app.

Adding rate limiting

We'll use the Quart extension called Quart-Rate-Limiter to enforce rate limits, which is installed by running the following command in the *backend* directory:

```
pdm add quart-rate-limiter
```

We can now activate `RateLimiter` by adding the following code to *backend/src/backend/run.py*:

```
from quart_rate_limiter import RateLimiter


rate_limiter = RateLimiter(app)
```

With the `RateLimiter` activated, any route in the app can be given **rate limit** protection, for example, to limit to six requests per minute, as follows:

```
from datetime import timedelta


from quart_rate_limiter import rate_limit


@app.get("/")
@rate_limit(6, timedelta(minutes=1))
async def handler():
    ...
```

As with other errors, it is important to provide a JSON response if the client exceeds the rate limit; we can do this by adding the following code to *backend/src/backend/run.py*:

```
from quart_rate_limiter import RateLimitExceeded


@app.errorhandler(RateLimitExceeded)  # type: ignore
async def handle_rate_limit_exceeded_error(
    error: RateLimitExceeded,
) -> ResponseReturnValue:
    return {}, error.get_headers(), 429
```

Now that we can add rate limits, it is best practice to add them to all of the routes. To ensure that we do so, let's add a test that checks for us.

Ensuring all routes have rate limits

Malicious attackers often search for paths with missing rate limits as a weakness they can then attack. To mitigate against this, I like to check that all routes have rate limits or are marked as exempt using the `rate_exempt` decorator. To do this, I add the following code to *tests/test_rate_limits.py*:

```
from quart_rate_limiter import (
    QUART_RATE_LIMITER_EXEMPT_ATTRIBUTE,
    QUART_RATE_LIMITER_LIMITS_ATTRIBUTE,
```

```
)

from backend.run import app

IGNORED_ENDPOINTS = {"static"}

def test_routes_have_rate_limits() -> None:
    for rule in app.url_map.iter_rules():
        endpoint = rule.endpoint

        exempt = getattr(
            app.view_functions[endpoint],
            QUART_RATE_LIMITER_EXEMPT_ATTRIBUTE,
            False,
        )
        if not exempt and endpoint not in IGNORED_ENDPOINTS:
            rate_limits = getattr(
                app.view_functions[endpoint],
                QUART_RATE_LIMITER_LIMITS_ATTRIBUTE,
                [],
            )
            assert rate_limits != []
```

In a Quart app, the rules are the method-path combinations that the app will respond to. Each rule has an endpoint that indicates which function should handle the request. The static endpoint is added by Quart, and hence we ignore it in this test.

This test will check that all of the routes in the app have a rate limit or are exempt. This means that we also need to add the `rate_exempt` decorator to the control ping endpoint we added when setting up the basic app. This is done by adding the highlighted decorator to the ping route handler in *backend/src/backend/blueprints/control.py* as follows:

```
from quart_rate_limiter import rate_exempt

@blueprint.get("/control/ping/")
@rate_exempt
async def ping() -> ResponseReturnValue:
    return {"ping": "pong"}
```

Alongside rate limiting routes, we can also protect the routes by validating the request and response data.

Adding request and response validation

Malicious users will often try to send malformed and invalid data in order to find mistakes in our code. To mitigate against this, we'll use the Quart extension called Quart-Schema to validate requests and responses. It is installed by running the following command in the *backend* directory:

```
pdm add "pydantic[email]"
pdm add quart-schema
```

By convention, JSON (Javascript/TypeScript) and Python use different naming conventions, with the former using *camelCase* and the latter *snake_case*. This means that we will need to convert between the two when receiving or replying. Fortunately, Quart-Schema can do this automatically for us, without any additional thought, via the convert_casing option.

We can activate QuartSchema, including setting the convert_casing option, by adding the following code to *backend/src/backend/run.py*:

```
from quart_schema import QuartSchema

schema = QuartSchema(app, convert_casing=True)
```

With this setup, we can use dataclass to define and validate the data the route expects to receive and to validate that it sends the correct data back, as follows:

```
from quart_schema import validate_request, validate_response

@dataclass
class Todo:
    task: str
    due: Optional[datetime]

@app.post("/")
@validate_request(Todo)
@validate_response(Todo)
async def create_todo(data: Todo) -> Todo:
    ...
    return data
```

As with other errors, it is important to provide a JSON response to the client with an informative message if the client sends the wrong data. We can do this by adding the following error handler to *backend/src/backend/run.py*:

```
from quart_schema import RequestSchemaValidationError


@app.errorhandler(RequestSchemaValidationError)  # type: ignore
async def handle_request_validation_error(
    error: RequestSchemaValidationError,
) -> ResponseReturnValue:
    if isinstance(error.validation_error, TypeError):
        return {"errors": str(error.validation_error)}, 400
    else:
        return {"errors": error.validation_error.json()}, 400
```

Checking the type of `validation_error` allows for useful information to be returned in the response, thereby helping correct the issue.

As Quart-Schema adds routes to our app that are not rate limited, we will need to change the `IGNORED_ENDPOINTS` line in *backend/tests/test_rate_limits.py* as follows:

```
IGNORED_ENDPOINTS = {"static", "openapi", "redoc_ui", "swagger_
ui"}
```

As we can validate the structure of the data sent and received by the backend, we can now turn to how we store the data in the database. For that, we will need to be able to connect to it and execute queries.

Connecting to the database

We have chosen to store the data the app needs in a PostgreSQL database, which we will need to connect to. To do this, I like to use the Quart extension called Quart-DB, which is a great wrapper around fast lower-level PostgreSQL drivers. It is installed by running the following command in the *backend* directory:

```
pdm add quart-db
```

We can activate `QuartDB` by adding the following code to *backend/src/backend/run.py*:

```
from quart_db import QuartDB


quart_db = QuartDB(app)
```

We also need to configure which database QuartDB should connect to. This is achieved by adding a TOZO_QUART_DB_DATABASE_URL environment variable, the value of which is constructed as follows, with the highlighted parts being configurable:

postgresql://**username:password**@0.0.0.0:5432/**db_name**

We'll use tozo for the username, password, and database name in development as they are very obvious and easy to remember. To do this, add the following to *backend/development.env*:

**TOZO_QUART_DB_DATABASE_URL="postgresql://
tozo:tozo@0.0.0.0:5432/tozo"**

When testing, we'll use tozo_test for the username, password, and database name so that test and development data are kept separate. To do this, add the following to *backend/testing.env*:

**TOZO_QUART_DB_DATABASE_URL="postgresql://tozo_test:tozo_
test@0.0.0.0:5432/tozo_test"**

As we develop, we will need to reset the database to a known state after making and testing changes. We'll also want to reset the database before running the tests to ensure the tests don't fail because the database is in a different state. To do this, we'll start by adding a Quart CLI command to recreate the database by adding the following code to *backend/src/backend/run.py*:

```python
import os
from subprocess import call  # nosec
from urllib.parse import urlparse


@app.cli.command("recreate_db")
def recreate_db() -> None:
    db_url = urlparse(os.environ["TOZO_QUART_DB_DATABASE_URL"])
    call(  # nosec
        ["psql", "-U", "postgres", "-c", f"DROP DATABASE IF
            EXISTS {db_url.path.removeprefix('/')}"],
    )
    call(  # nosec
        ["psql", "-U", "postgres", "-c", f"DROP USER IF EXISTS
            {db_url.username}"],
    )
    call(  # nosec
        ["psql", "-U", "postgres", "-c", f"CREATE USER {db_url.
        username} LOGIN PASSWORD '{db_url.password}' CREATEDB"],
```

```
    )
    call(  # nosec
        ["psql", "-U", "postgres", "-c", f"CREATE DATABASE {db_
          url.path.removeprefix('/')}"],
    )
```

This command calls out to `psql` using the `call` function. The first two calls will drop the database and user if they already exist using the DROP DATABASE and DROP USER SQL commands. After they've been dropped, the next calls create the user and then the database using the CREATE USER and CREATE DATABASE SQL commands.

We can now utilize this command in the `pdm run test` script and add a new `pdm run recreate-db` script to reset the database on demand by making the following change to *backend/pyproject.toml*:

```
[tool.pdm.scripts]
recreate-db-base = "quart --app src/backend/run.py recreate_db"
recreate-db = {composite = ["recreate-db-base"], env_file =
  "development.env"}
test = {composite = ["recreate-db-base", "pytest tests/"], env_
  file = "testing.env"}
```

The highlighted line indicates that the `test` script has been changed, whereas the `recreate-db` and `recreate-db-base` scripts have been added.

To check whether this works, we can now create the development database by running the following command in the *backend* directory:

```
pdm run recreate-db
```

Then, to check that it has worked, we can open a `psql` shell to the database with the following command:

```
psql -U tozo
```

The preceding command should give an output similar to that in *Figure 2.3*:

Figure 2.3: The output from psql when running the \dt command to describe the empty database

> **PSQL**
>
> PSQL is a command-line tool that can connect to a PostgreSQL database and allows queries and other commands to be run. This means you can test SQL queries from the command line and inspect the structure of the database. I'd recommend you try the `\dt` command that lists all of the tables in the database, and the `\d tbl` command that describes the structure of the table called *tbl*.

When testing, we'll need to run our tests in the Quart test app context as this ensures that the database connection is established. To do so, we need to add the following code to *backend/tests/conftest.py*:

```python
from typing import AsyncGenerator

import pytest
from quart import Quart

from backend.run import app

@pytest.fixture(name="app", scope="function")
async def _app() -> AsyncGenerator[Quart, None]:
    async with app.test_app():
        yield app
```

The `pytest` fixtures can be injected into tests, which means that we can use this fixture in our tests by declaring it as an argument. This means that *backend/tests/blueprints/test_control.py* must be rewritten as follows:

```python
from quart import Quart

async def test_control(app: Quart) -> None:
    test_client = app.test_client()
    response = await test_client.get("/control/ping/")
    assert (await response.get_json())["ping"] == "pong"
```

Another useful feature would be a direct connection to the database to use in the tests. This fixture is provided by adding the following code to *backend/conftest.py*:

```python
from quart_db import Connection

from backend.run import quart_db
```

```
@pytest.fixture(name="connection", scope="function")
async def _connection(app: Quart) -> AsyncGenerator[Connection,
None]:
    async with quart_db.connection() as connection:
        async with connection.transaction():
            yield connection
```

With this in place, all of our tests can use the app fixture and run tests against the testing database.

Alongside connecting to the database, we will also need the backend to connect to an email server to send emails to the users.

Sending emails

We will want to send users of our app emails, with the first being a confirmation email when they register. Another will be sent if the user forgets their password, as we can send them a password reset email. These targeted emails are transactional rather than marketing in nature, which is an important distinction as marketing emails are rarely sent via the app code.

With **transactional emails**, the aim is usually to convey a task to the user as clearly as possible. For this reason, the emails are usually text-based with minimal imagery. However, we should ensure the email is branded and has space for any required legal text. This means that we need to render the emails so that the transactional text is clear and surrounded by relevant branding and text.

Rendering emails

We will consider an email as consisting of a header where we will place branding (such as a logo), content where the specifics of the email (for example, a link to our app's password reset page) are placed, and a footer where any legal information is placed. As only the content changes between emails, we can consider rendering the header and footer separately to the content.

As most email clients support HTML, we can style our emails to make them more engaging and pleasant to read. This means that we will need a HTML header/footer into which we can render the content of the specific email. This is best done using Quart's built-in render_template function, which utilizes Jinja2 to render template documents.

To start with the header and footer, we need to place the following code in *backend/src/backend/templates/email.html*:

```
<!DOCTYPE html>
<html>
  <head>
    <title>Tozo - email</title>
```

```
    <meta http-equiv="Content-Type" content="text/html;
      charset=UTF-8">
    <meta name="viewport" content="width=device-width, initial-
      scale=1.0">
</head>

<body style="font-family: Arial, 'Helvetica Neue', Helvetica,
 sans-serif; font-size: 14px; font-style: normal; margin: 0">
  <table width="100%" height="100%" cellpadding="0"
    cellspacing="0" border="0">
    <tr>
      <td align="center">
        <table height="100%" cellpadding="20" cellspacing="0"
          border="0" style="max-width: 540px;">
          <tr>
            <td align="left" width="540">
              {% block welcome %}
                Hello,
              {% endblock %}
            </td>
          </tr>
          <tr>
            <td align="left" width="540">
              {% block content %}
                Example content
              {% endblock %}
            </td>
          </tr>
          <tr>
            <td align="center" width="540">
              The Tozo team
            </td>
          </tr>
        </table>
      </td>
    </tr>
  </table>
```

```
    </body>
</html>
```

As email clients only support limited parts of HTML and CSS, we are using a table to lay out the email. The layout we are aiming for is where the content is kept within a width of 540 px in the center of the viewport. This should support the majority of email clients while still looking good.

The highlighted `block` directives show only the contents within them when rendered, as shown in *Figure 2.4*. It allows any template that extends this base email to replace the contents of the blocks, hence we'll use this as a base for all our emails.

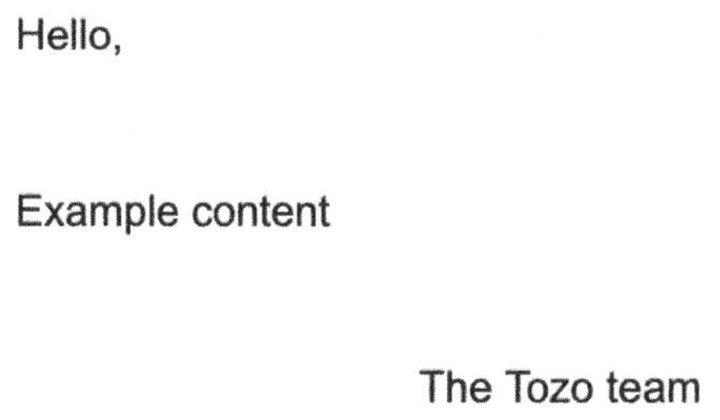

Hello,

Example content

The Tozo team

Figure 2.4: The rendered email when viewed in a browser

---

caniemail.com

The `caniemail.com` website is an invaluable resource for checking which HTML and CSS features are supported by the various email clients in existence. I would recommend checking this site for any features added to the HTML email.

Now that we have nice-looking emails, we can add code to send them to the user's email address.

Sending emails

While it is possible to send emails directly from the app using a SMTP server, I find that it is better practice to use a third-party service such as Postmark (`https://postmarkapp.com`). This is because Postmark will ensure that our emails are sent reliably from a setup that helps ensure a low spam score, which is hard to achieve from a new SMTP server.

In development and testing, I prefer not to send emails but rather just log them out. I find this makes development easier and quicker (no checking any email inboxes). We can do this by starting with a `send_email` function that logs the email to the console by adding the following code to *backend/ src/backend/lib/email.py*:

```
import logging
from typing import Any
```

```
from quart import render_template

log = logging.getLogger(__name__)

async def send_email(
    to: str,
    subject: str,
    template: str,
    ctx: dict[str, Any],
) -> None:
    content = await render_template(template, **ctx)
    log.info("Sending %s to %s\n%s", template, to, content)
```

We'll also need to configure the logging, which we can do with a basic setup by adding the following code to *backend/src/backend/run.py*:

```
import logging

logging.basicConfig(level=logging.INFO)
```

To send emails with the third-party Postmark, we will need to send HTTP requests to their API. To do so, we can use httpx, which is installed by running the following command in the *backend* directory:

```
pdm add httpx
```

We can then adjust the send_email function to send via Postmark if a token is available in the configuration by changing the code in *backend/src/backend/lib/email.py* as follows:

```
import logging
from typing import Any, cast

import httpx
from quart import current_app, render_template

log = logging.getLogger(__name__)

class PostmarkError(Exception):
    def __init__(self, error_code: int, message: str) -> None:
```

```python
        self.error_code = error_code
        self.message = message


async def send_email(
    to: str,
    subject: str,
    template: str,
    ctx: dict[str, Any],
) -> None:
    content = await render_template(template, **ctx)
    log.info("Sending %s to %s\n%s", template, to, content)
    token = current_app.config.get("POSTMARK_TOKEN")
    if token is not None:
        async with httpx.AsyncClient() as client:
            response = await client.post(
                "https://api.postmarkapp.com/email",
                json={
                    "From": "Tozo <help@tozo.dev>",
                    "To": to,
                    "Subject": subject,
                    "Tag": template,
                    "HtmlBody": content,
                },
                headers={"X-Postmark-Server-Token": token},
            )
        data = cast(dict, response.json())
        if response.status_code != 200:
            raise PostmarkError(
                data["ErrorCode"], data["Message"]
            )
```

The send_email function now uses httpx to send a post request to Postmark, including the required token as a header and the email content in the request JSON body. Any errors returned by Postmark are raised as an easily identified PostmarkError. We can now focus on how we can use emails in the tests.

Testing that emails are sent

When testing functionality in the backend, we'll often want to check that an email was sent. We can do this by testing the send_email function by adding the following code to *backend/tests/lib/test_email.py*:

```
from pytest import LogCaptureFixture
from quart import Quart

from backend.lib.email import send_email

async def test_send_email(
    app: Quart, caplog: LogCaptureFixture
) -> None:
    async with app.app_context():
        await send_email(
            "member@tozo.dev", "Welcome", "email.html", {}
        )
    assert "Sending email.html to member@tozo.dev" in caplog.
text
```

caplog is a pytest fixture that captures everything that is logged during the test. This allows us to check that our email was logged by looking for the specific text.

With the backend now set up, we have everything we need in place to start developing our app's API. The folder structure at this stage is as follows:

```
tozo
├── .github
│   └── workflows
├── backend
│   ├── src
│   │   └── backend
│   │       └── blueprints
│   │       └── lib
│   │       └── templates
│   └── tests
│       └── backend
│           └── blueprints
│           └── lib
│
```

```
├── frontend
│     ├── public
│     └── src
└── infrastructure
```

Summary

In this chapter, we've built a backend app in Quart that we can build our specific API on. It can connect to the database, manage user sessions, protect itself against heavy and incorrect usage, and send emails to the users.

The features we've built in this chapter are common to many apps, and hence they will be useful for the app you are trying to build. In addition, the backend built in this chapter is generic and can be adapted for your specific use.

In the following chapter, we'll add an API to manage the users, allow users to log in, and support the to-do functionality we are building in this book.

Further reading

We've chosen to send only HTML emails for simplicity in this book; however, it is better practice to send multipart emails with HTML and plain-text parts. You can read an advocacy for this at `https://useplaintext.email`.

3
Building the API

In the previous chapter, we built a backend that connects to the database, manages user sessions, and sends emails. Now, we will add a specific API to the backend that tracks the member's to-do's. This will require an API that allows members, sessions, and to-dos to be managed.

In this chapter, you'll learn how to build a **RESTful API**, which is a very popular style of API and one you'll likely use and come across in your career. You'll also build an API to manage members and authenticate their actions, which could be used in any other app with minimal changes. Finally, we will also build an API to track the to-dos, which, again, could be adapted for other uses.

We'll build the API using a RESTful style as it works very well with web apps and can be expressed very easily with Quart. A RESTful API is where the functionality is grouped by resource with each function being an action acting on the resource. For example, the functionality to log in is described as creating a session and log out as deleting a session. For a RESTful web app, the action is represented by the HTTP verb and the resource by the HTTP path. In addition, the response status code is used to indicate the effect of the functionality, with 2XX codes indicating success and 4XX codes indicating different types of errors.

Alternatives to RESTful APIs

While RESTful APIs utilize many HTTP verbs and paths to describe the functionality, a more basic style is to have a singular POST route. This route is then used for all the functionality with the request body describing the function and data. A good example is GraphQL, which typically uses only POST /graphql with a defined message structure. If you'd prefer to use GraphQL take a look at https://strawberry.rocks.

So, in this chapter, we will cover the following topics:

- Creating the database schema and models

- Building the session API

- Building the member API

- Building the to-do API

Technical requirements

The following additional folders are required in this chapter and should be created:

```
tozo
└── backend
    ├── src
    │   └── backend
    │       ├── migrations
    │       └── models
    └── tests
        └── models
```

Empty *backend/src/backend/models/__init__.py* and *backend/tests/models/__init__.py* files should also be created.

To follow the development in this chapter, use the companion repository, `https://github.com/pgjones/tozo`, and see the commits between the tags `r1-ch3-start` and `r1-ch3-end`.

Creating the database schema and models

In this book, we are building a to-do tracking app, which means we need to store data about the member and their to-dos. We will do so by placing the data into the database, which means we need to define the structure of the data. This structure is called the schema and describes the tables in the database.

While the **schema** describes the structure of the data in the database, we will use models in the backend and frontend. Each model is a class that represents a row in the database. For example, a table with only an ID could be represented by a class with a single `id` attribute.

> **ORMs**
> Schemas and models are often conflated as the same thing, especially when an **Object Relational Model (ORM)** is used. While using an ORM is simpler to begin with, I find it hides important details and makes development harder after a short while. This is why, in this book, the model and schema are related but different. This also means that we'll write SQL queries for all interactions with the database.

We'll start by defining the member data and to-do data as both models and schemas in a migration, before adding some initial test and development data.

Creating the member schema and model

We need to store information for each member so that we can associate their to-dos with them, via a foreign key reference. In addition, we need to store enough information so that the member can log in and prove who they are (authenticate themselves), which means we need to store their email and password hash. Finally, we'll also store when their account was created and when they verified their email – the latter being important if we want to send them emails.

The schema for this data is given by the following SQL, which is given for reference and will be used in the *Running the first migration* section:

```
CREATE TABLE members (
    id INT PRIMARY KEY GENERATED ALWAYS AS IDENTITY,
    created TIMESTAMP NOT NULL DEFAULT now(),
    email TEXT NOT NULL,
    email_verified TIMESTAMP,
    password_hash TEXT NOT NULL
);


CREATE UNIQUE INDEX members_unique_email_idx on members
(LOWER(email));
```

The unique index highlighted ensures that there is only one member account per email, with email casing being ignored.

> **SQL formatting**
>
> In *Chapter 1 Setting Up Our System for Development*, I mentioned the importance of code formatting and autoformatters. Sadly, I haven't found an autoformatter that works for SQL embedded in Python code. However, I recommend you follow the style guide given at http://sqlstyle.guide/ as I will in this book.

We can represent the database table with a Python `dataclass`, which includes each column as an attribute with the relevant Python type. This is the model shown in the following code, which should be added to *backend/src/backend/models/member.py*:

```
from dataclasses import dataclass
from datetime import datetime
```

```python
@dataclass
class Member:
    id: int
    email: str
    password_hash: str
    created: datetime
    email_verified: datetime | None
```

In addition to the model, we can add the following functions to *backend/src/backend/models/member. py* in order to convert between the backend model and the SQL that reads from the database:

```python
from quart_db import Connection


async def select_member_by_email(
    db: Connection, email: str
) -> Member | None:
    result = await db.fetch_one(
        """SELECT id, email, password_hash, created,
                  email_verified
             FROM members
            WHERE LOWER(email) = LOWER(:email)""",
        {"email": email},
    )
    return None if result is None else Member(**result)


async def select_member_by_id(
    db: Connection, id: int
) -> Member | None:
    result = await db.fetch_one(
        """SELECT id, email, password_hash, created,
                  email_verified
             FROM members
            WHERE id = :id""",
        {"id": id},
    )
    return None if result is None else Member(**result)
```

These functions allow member information to be read from the database. The highlighted line ensures that emails are considered a match if the lowercased email matches.

Email case sensitivity

In our app, we store the email in the case given by the user, while comparing lowercased emails. This is the most user-friendly and secure solution, as emails can have a case-sensitive local part (before the @) but rarely do and must be case insensitive for the domain part (after the @). Therefore, by storing the given casing we ensure the email is delivered while ensuring there is one account per email address. More information is available at `https://stackoverflow.com/questions/9807909/are-email-addresses-case-sensitive`.

Next, we need to add functions that can alter the data in the database by adding the following to *backend/src/models/member.py*:

```python
async def insert_member(
    db: Connection, email: str, password_hash: str
) -> Member:
    result = await db.fetch_one(
        """INSERT INTO members (email, password_hash)
                VALUES (:email, :password_hash)
            RETURNING id, email, password_hash, created,
                    email_verified""",
        {"email": email, "password_hash": password_hash},
    )
    return Member(**result)


async def update_member_password(
    db: Connection, id: int, password_hash: str
) -> None:
    await db.execute(
        """UPDATE members
                SET password_hash = :password_hash
            WHERE id = :id""",
        {"id": id, "password_hash": password_hash},
    )


async def update_member_email_verified(
    db: Connection, id: int
```

```
) -> None:
    await db.execute(
        "UPDATE members SET email_verified = now() WHERE id =
:id",
        {"id": id},
    )
```

These functions match the functionality we'll shortly add to the API.

The case sensitivity is something we should test, by adding the following to *backend/tests/models/test_member.py*:

```
import pytest
from asyncpg.exceptions import UniqueViolationError  # type:
ignore
from quart_db import Connection

from backend.models.member import insert_member

async def test_insert_member(connection: Connection) -> None:
    await insert_member(connection, "casing@tozo.dev", "")
    with pytest.raises(UniqueViolationError):
        await insert_member(connection, "Casing@tozo.dev", "")
```

Firstly, we want a test to ensure that insert_member correctly rejects a second member with an email that differs only by casing. The highlighted line ensures that the lines within, when executed, raise a UniqueViolationError and hence prevents the member from being inserted again.

We also need to test that the select_member_by_email function compares case insensitively by adding the following to *backend/tests/models/test_member.py*:

```
from backend.models.member import select_member_by_email

async def test_select_member_by_email (connection: Connection)
-> None:
    await insert_member(connection, "casing@tozo.dev", "")
    member = await select_member_by_email(
        connection, "Casing@tozo.dev"
    )
    assert member is not None
```

With the model code set up this way, we'll be able to use these functions and the class instance directly wherever required in the backend code.

Creating the to-do schema and model

We also want to store information for each to-do, specifically the to-do task as text, when the to-do is due to be completed (although this should be optional), and if the to-do is complete. In addition, every to-do should be linked to the member that owns it.

The schema for this data is given by the following SQL, which is given for reference and will be used in the *Running the first migration* section:

```sql
CREATE TABLE todos (
    id BIGINT PRIMARY KEY GENERATED ALWAYS AS IDENTITY,
    complete BOOLEAN NOT NULL DEFAULT FALSE,
    due TIMESTAMPTZ,
    member_id INT NOT NULL REFERENCES members(id),
    task TEXT NOT NULL
);
```

The corresponding backend model for this table is given by the following code, which should be added to *backend/src/backend/models/todo.py*:

```python
from dataclasses import dataclass
from datetime import datetime

from pydantic import constr


@dataclass
class Todo:
    complete: bool
    due: datetime | None
    id: int
    task: constr(strip_whitespace=True, min_length=1)  # type:
ignore
```

Here, `constr` is used in place of `str` in order to ensure that empty strings are not considered valid. In addition to the model, we can add the following functions to *backend/src/backend/models/todo.py* in order to convert between the backend model and the SQL that reads from the database:

```python
from quart_db import Connection


async def select_todos(
    connection: Connection,
    member_id: int,
    complete: bool | None = None,
) -> list[Todo]:
    if complete is None:
        query = """SELECT id, complete, due, task
                     FROM todos
                    WHERE member_id = :member_id"""
        values = {"member_id": member_id}
    else:
        query = """SELECT id, complete, due, task
                     FROM todos
                    WHERE member_id = :member_id
                      AND complete = :complete"""
        values = {"member_id": member_id, "complete": complete}
    return [
        Todo(**row)
        async for row in connection.iterate(query, values)
    ]


async def select_todo(
    connection: Connection, id: int, member_id: int,
) -> Todo | None:
    result = await connection.fetch_one(
        """SELECT id, complete, due, task
             FROM todos
            WHERE id = :id AND member_id = :member_id""",
        {"id": id, "member_id": member_id},
    )
    return None if result is None else Todo(**result)
```

These functions allow to-dos to be read from the database, but will only return to-dos that are owned by the given `member_id`. Using these functions should ensure that we don't return to-dos to the wrong members.

Next, we need to add functions that can alter the data in the database by adding the following to *backend/src/models/todo.py*:

```python
async def insert_todo(
    connection: Connection,
    member_id: int,
    task: str,
    complete: bool,
    due: datetime | None,
) -> Todo:
    result = await connection.fetch_one(
        """INSERT INTO todos (complete, due, member_id, task)
                VALUES (:complete, :due, :member_id, :task)
             RETURNING id, complete, due, task""",
        {
            "member_id": member_id,
            "task": task,
            "complete": complete,
            "due": due,
        },
    )
    return Todo(**result)


async def update_todo(
    connection: Connection,
    id: int,
    member_id: int,
    task: str,
    complete: bool,
    due: datetime | None,
) -> Todo | None:
    result = await connection.fetch_one(
        """UPDATE todos
                SET complete = :complete, due = :due,
```

```
            task = :task
        WHERE id = :id AND member_id = :member_id
    RETURNING id, complete, due, task""",
        {
            "id": id,
            "member_id": member_id,
            "task": task,
            "complete": complete,
            "due": due,
        },
    )
    return None if result is None else Todo(**result)


async def delete_todo(
    connection: Connection, id: int, member_id: int,
) -> None:
    await connection.execute(
        "DELETE FROM todos WHERE id = :id AND member_id =
:member_id",
        {"id": id, "member_id": member_id},
    )
```

Note that all these functions also take a member_id argument and only affect the to-dos that belong to the given member_id. This will help us avoid authorization errors whereby we write code that mistakenly allows a member to access or modify another member's to-do.

This is something we should test, by adding the following to *backend/tests/models/test_todo.py*. Firstly, we want a test to ensure that delete_todo correctly deletes the to-do:

```
import pytest
from quart_db import Connection

from backend.models.todo import (
    delete_todo, insert_todo, select_todo, update_todo
)


@pytest.mark.parametrize(
    "member_id, deleted",
```

```
    [(1, True), (2, False)],
)
async def test_delete_todo(
    connection: Connection, member_id: int, deleted: bool
) -> None:
    todo = await insert_todo(
        connection, 1, "Task", False, None
    )
    await delete_todo(connection, todo.id, member_id)
    new_todo = await select_todo(connection, todo.id, 1)
    assert (new_todo is None) is deleted
```

The highlighted parametrization provides two tests. The first test ensures that member_id 1 can delete their to-do, and the second test ensures that member_id 2 cannot delete another user's to-do.

We should also add a similar test to ensure that the update works as expected:

```
@pytest.mark.parametrize(
    "member_id, complete",
    [(1, True), (2, False)],
)
async def test_update_todo(
    connection: Connection, member_id: int, complete: bool
) -> None:
    todo = await insert_todo(
        connection, 1, "Task", False, None
    )
    await update_todo(
        connection, todo.id, member_id, "Task", True, None
    )
    new_todo = await select_todo(connection, todo.id, 1)
    assert new_todo is not None
    assert new_todo.complete is complete
```

The parametrization provides two tests. The first test ensures that the member with member_id 1 can update their to-do, and the second test ensures that the member with member_id 2 can update another user's to-do.

While we have these important tests in place, we can't run them until we create the datab via a migration.

Running the first migration

While we've written the SQL queries required to create the database schema, they haven't run against the database. To run these, Quart-DB provides a migration system, whereby we can run queries as the backend starts, but only if they haven't already run. To make use of this, we can add the following code to *backend/src/backend/migrations/0.py*:

```python
from quart_db import Connection

async def migrate(connection: Connection) -> None:
    await connection.execute(
        """CREATE TABLE members (
            id INT PRIMARY KEY GENERATED ALWAYS AS IDENTITY,
            created TIMESTAMP NOT NULL DEFAULT now(),
            email TEXT NOT NULL,
            email_verified TIMESTAMP,
            password_hash TEXT NOT NULL
        )""",
    )
    await connection.execute(
        """CREATE UNIQUE INDEX members_unique_email_idx
                    ON members (LOWER(email)
        )"""
    )
    await connection.execute(
        """CREATE TABLE todos (
            id BIGINT PRIMARY KEY GENERATED ALWAYS AS
                IDENTITY,
            complete BOOLEAN NOT NULL DEFAULT FALSE,
            ⎺⎺MESTAMPTZ,
            d INT NOT NULL REFERENCES members(id),
            T NOT NULL
```

ase tables

ation(connection: Connection) -> bool:

To see this migration take effect, you can run `pdm run recreate-db` and then start the backend (as the migration will run as the backend starts up). You can then use `psql -U tozo` to inspect the database and see the two new tables as shown in *Figure 3.1*:

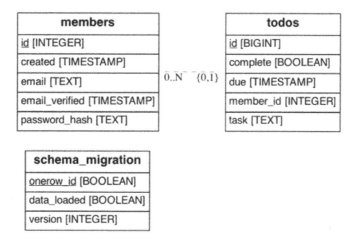

Figure 3.1: The database schema after the migration.

There is a one-to-many relationship between the `members` and `todos` tables such that one member has many to-dos. Also note the `schema_migration` table is created and managed by Quart-DB to track migrations.

Adding test and development data

It is helpful to have some standardized initial data in the database when developing and running tests; for example, we can add a standard member with known credentials to log in, rather than have to create a new member every time the database is recreated. To do this, we can utilize the data path feature in Quart-DB.

For ease of use, we'll add a single member to the database by adding the following to *backend/src/backend/migrations/data.py*:

```
from quart_db import Connection


async def execute(connection: Connection) -> None:
    await connection.execute(
        """INSERT INTO members (email, password_hash)
                VALUES ('member@tozo.dev',
'$2b$14$6yXjNza30kPCg3LhzZJfqeCWOLM.zyTiQFD4rdWlFHBTfYzzKJMJe'
            ) """
```

```
    )
    await connection.execute(
        """INSERT INTO todos (member_id, task)
                VALUES (1, 'Test Task')"""
    )
```

The password hash value corresponds to a value of `password`, which means the login will be with the email, password combination of `member@tozo.dev`, `password`.

To instruct Quart-DB to load and run this file, we need to add the following configuration variable to *backend/development.env* and *backend/testing.env*:

```
TOZO_QUART_DB_DATA_PATH="migrations/data.py"
```

We can now run the tests and check that they pass by running the following in the *backend* directory:

```
pdm run test
```

Now we've defined the data stored by the backend, we can focus on the API, starting with session management.

Building the session API

To manage user sessions, we need a **session** (authentication) API that provides routes to log in and log out (i.e., to create and delete sessions). Login should result in a cookie being set, and logout results in the cookie being deleted. As per the authentication setup, login should require an email and matching password. We'll add this API via a sessions blueprint containing login, logout, and status functionality.

Creating the blueprint

A blueprint is a collection of route handlers and is useful to associate the related session functionality. It can be created with the following code in *backend/src/backend/blueprints/sessions.py*:

```
from quart import Blueprint

blueprint = Blueprint("sessions", __name__)
```

The blueprint then needs to be registered with the app, by adding the following to *backend/src/backend/run.py*:

```
from backend.blueprints.sessions import blueprint as sessions_
blueprint


app.register_blueprint(sessions_blueprint)
```

With the blueprint created, we can now add specific functionality as routes.

Adding login functionality

The login functionality is described in a RESTful style as creating a session, and hence the route should be POST, expecting an email, a password, and a remember flag returning 200 on success and 401 on invalid credentials. This is done via the following, which should be added to *backend/src/backend/blueprints/sessions.py*:

```
from dataclasses import dataclass
from datetime import timedelta

import bcrypt
from pydantic import EmailStr
from quart import g, ResponseReturnValue
from quart_auth import AuthUser, login_user
from quart_rate_limiter import rate_limit
from quart_schema import validate_request

from backend.lib.api_error import APIError
from backend.models.member import select_member_by_email

@dataclass
class LoginData:
    email: EmailStr
    password: str
    remember: bool = False

@blueprint.post("/sessions/")
@rate_limit(5, timedelta(minutes=1))
@validate_request(LoginData)
```

```
async def login(data: LoginData) -> ResponseReturnValue:
    """Login to the app.

    By providing credentials and then saving the
    returned cookie.
    """
    result = await select_member_by_email(
        g.connection, data.email
    )
    if result is None:
        raise APIError(401, "INVALID_CREDENTIALS")

    passwords_match = bcrypt.checkpw(
        data.password.encode("utf-8"),
        result.password_hash.encode("utf-8"),
    )
    if passwords_match:
        login_user(AuthUser(str(result.id)), data.remember)
        return {}, 200
    else:
        raise APIError(401, "INVALID_CREDENTIALS")
```

This route is rate limited to a lower limit than others (five requests a minute) to prevent malicious actors from brute forcing the login. This is where the malicious actor keeps trying different passwords in the hope that one will eventually be correct and allow login.

The route also validates the request data has the correct LoginData structure, which ensures that users correctly use this route, and prevents invalid data from causing errors in the route handler code.

The route itself tries to fetch the member's details from the database given the email provided in the request data. If there is no data, a 401 response is returned. The password provided in the request data is then checked against the password hash in the database, with a match resulting in the member being logged in with a 200 response. If the passwords don't match, a 401 response is returned.

Trailing slashes

For this route, and for all others in the app, I've added a trailing slash so that the path is /sessions/ rather than /sessions. This is a useful convention to follow as requests to /sessions will be automatically redirected to /sessions/ and hence work despite the missing slash, whereas requests to /sessions/ would not be redirected to /session if the route was defined without the trailing slash.

Logging in results in a cookie being stored in the member's browser, which is then sent in every subsequent request. The presence and value of this cookie are used to determine whether the member is logged in, and which member made the request.

> **Account enumeration**
>
> This implementation will allow an attacker to enumerate emails present in the database, which can be considered a security issue. See *Chapter 7, Securing and Packaging the App*, for how to mitigate against this.

Adding logout functionality

A logout route is described as a session deletion in a RESTful style, therefore the route should be DELETE, returning 200. The following should be added to *backend/src/backend/blueprints/sessions.py*:

```
from quart_auth import logout_user
from quart_rate_limiter import rate_exempt


@blueprint.delete("/sessions/")
@rate_exempt
async def logout() -> ResponseReturnValue:
    """Logout from the app.

    Deletes the session cookie.
    """
    logout_user()
    return {}
```

This route is rate exempt as nothing should prevent a member from logging out – it is important that the logout function works so that members are logged out when they want to be. The route then only needs to call `logout_user`, which results in the cookie being deleted.

> **Idempotent routes**
>
> Idempotence is a property of a route where the final state is achieved no matter how many times the route is called, that is, calling the route once or 10 times has the same effect. This is a useful property as it means the route can be safely retried if the request fails. For RESTful and HTTP APIs, the routes using GET, PUT, and DELETE verbs are expected to be idempotent. In this book, the routes using the GET, PUT, and DELETE verbs are idempotent.

Adding status functionality

It is useful to have a route that returns the current session (status) as we'll use it for debugging and testing. For a RESTful API, this should be a GET route, and the following should be added to *backend/src/backend/blueprints/sessions.py*:

```python
from quart_auth import current_user, login_required
from quart_schema import validate_response

@dataclass
class Status:
    member_id: int

@blueprint.get("/sessions/")
@rate_limit(10, timedelta(minutes=1))
@login_required
@validate_response(Status)
async def status() -> ResponseReturnValue:
    assert current_user.auth_id is not None  # nosec
    return Status(member_id=int(current_user.auth_id))
```

The highlighted assertion is used to inform the type checker that `current_user.auth_id` cannot be None in this function, and hence prevents the type checker from considering the subsequent line as an error. The `# nosec` comment informs the bandit security checker that this use of `assert` is not a security risk.

The route is rate limited for protection and will only run if the request has the correct cookie present from login. The route returns the member's ID based on the value in the cookie as this is also very useful.

Testing the routes

We should test that these routes work as a user would expect, starting by testing that a user can log in, get their status, and then log out as a complete flow. This is tested by adding the following to *backend/tests/blueprints/test_sessions.py*:

```python
from quart import Quart

async def test_session_flow(app: Quart) -> None:
    test_client = app.test_client()
    await test_client.post(
```

```
        "/sessions/",
        json={
            "email": "member@tozo.dev", "password": "password"
        },
    )
    response = await test_client.get("/sessions/")
    assert (await response.get_json())["memberId"] == 1
    await test_client.delete("/sessions/")
    response = await test_client.get("/sessions/")
    assert response.status_code == 401
```

This test ensures that a member can log in and then access routes that require them to be logged in. It then logs the member out and checks that they can no longer access the route.

We should also test that the login route returns the correct response if the wrong credentials are provided by adding the following test to *backend/tests/blueprints/test_sessions.py*:

```
async def test_login_invalid_password(app: Quart) -> None:
    test_client = app.test_client()
    await test_client.post(
        "/sessions/",
        json={
            "email": "member@tozo.dev", "password": "incorrect"
        },
    )
    response = await test_client.get("/sessions/")
    assert response.status_code == 401
```

This is all we need to allow members to log in and log out. Next, we can focus on managing members.

Building the member API

To manage members, we need an API that provides routes to create a member (register), confirm the email address, change the password, request a password reset, and reset a password.

We'll add this API via a blueprint for the member, containing registration, email confirmation, changing password, and password reset functionality.

Creating the members blueprint

To begin, we should create a blueprint for all the member routes, it is created with the following code in *backend/src/backend/blueprints/members.py*:

```
from quart import Blueprint


blueprint = Blueprint("members", __name__)
```

The blueprint then needs to be registered with the app, by adding the following to *backend/src/backend/run.py*:

```
from backend.blueprints.members import blueprint as members_
blueprint


app.register_blueprint(members_blueprint)
```

With the blueprint created, we can now add the specific functionality as routes.

Creating a member

In our app, we want users to be able to register as members. This requires a route that accepts an email and a password. The route should then check the password is sufficiently complex, create a new member, and send a welcome email. As the route creates a member, it should use the POST method to be in the RESTful style.

We'll add a link to the welcome email that the recipient of the email can visit to prove they registered with our app. This way, we have verified that the email address owner is the same user that registered. The link will work by including an authentication token in the path, with the token working as explained in *Chapter 2, Creating a Reusable Backend with Quart*.

We can do this by first creating an email template by adding the following to *backend/src/backend/templates/welcome.html*:

```
{% extends "email.html" %}

{% block welcome %}
  Hello and welcome to tozo!
{% endblock %}

{% block content %}
  Please confirm you signed up by following this
```

```
  <a href="{{ config['BASE_URL'] }}/confirm-email/{{ token
}}/">
    link
  </a>.
{% endblock %}
```

The route itself should return 201 on success, as this status code indicates a successful creation. This is all achieved by adding the following to *backend/src/backend/blueprints/members.py*:

```python
from dataclasses import dataclass
from datetime import timedelta

import asyncpg  # type: ignore
import bcrypt
from itsdangerous import URLSafeTimedSerializer
from quart import current_app, g, ResponseReturnValue
from quart_schema import validate_request
from quart_rate_limiter import rate_limit
from zxcvbn import zxcvbn  # type: ignore

from backend.lib.api_error import APIError
from backend.lib.email import send_email
from backend.models.member import insert_member

MINIMUM_STRENGTH = 3
EMAIL_VERIFICATION_SALT = "email verify"

@dataclass
class MemberData:
    email: str
    password: str

@blueprint.post("/members/")
@rate_limit(10, timedelta(seconds=10))
@validate_request(MemberData)
async def register(data: MemberData) -> ResponseReturnValue:
    """Create a new Member.
```

```
This allows a Member to be created.
"""
strength = zxcvbn(data.password)
if strength["score"] < MINIMUM_STRENGTH:
    raise APIError(400, "WEAK_PASSWORD")

hashed_password = bcrypt.hashpw(
    data.password.encode("utf-8"),
    bcrypt.gensalt(14),
)
try:
    member = await insert_member(
        g.connection,
        data.email,
        hashed_password.decode(),
    )
except asyncpg.exceptions.UniqueViolationError:
    pass
else:
    serializer = URLSafeTimedSerializer(
        current_app.secret_key,
        salt=EMAIL_VERIFICATION_SALT,
    )
    token = serializer.dumps(member.id)
    await send_email(
        member.email,
        "Welcome",
        "welcome.html",
        {"token": token},
    )

return {}, 201
```

As can be seen, the password strength is first checked, using zxcvbn, with weak passwords resulting in a 400 response. The password is then hashed and used with the email to insert a member. The new member's ID is then used to create an email verification token, which is rendered into the email body before being sent to the given email address.

When the user follows the link, they will return to our app with the token for the email confirmation route to check.

Confirming the email address

When a user registers as a member, they are sent a link back to our app that includes an email verification token. The token identifies the member and hence confirms that the email address is correct. Therefore, we need a route that accepts the token and, if valid, confirms the email address. This updates the member's email property in a RESTful sense and hence is achieved by adding the following to *backend/src/backend/blueprints/members.py*:

```python
from itsdangerous import BadSignature, SignatureExpired


from backend.models.member import update_member_email_verified


ONE_MONTH = int(timedelta(days=30).total_seconds())


@dataclass
class TokenData:
    token: str


@blueprint.put("/members/email/")
@rate_limit(5, timedelta(minutes=1))
@validate_request(TokenData)
async def verify_email(data: TokenData) -> ResponseReturnValue:
    """Call to verify an email.

    This requires the user to supply a valid token.
    """
    serializer = URLSafeTimedSerializer(
        current_app.secret_key, salt=EMAIL_VERIFICATION_SALT
    )
    try:
        member_id = serializer.loads(
            data.token, max_age=ONE_MONTH
        )
    except SignatureExpired:
        raise APIError(403, "TOKEN_EXPIRED")
```

```
except BadSignature:
    raise APIError(400, "TOKEN_INVALID")
else:
    await update_member_email_verified(g.connection,
        member_id)
return {}
```

The token is checked via the loads method, and if it is expired a 403 response is returned, whereas if it is invalid a 400 response is returned. If the token is good, the member's email is marked as verified in the database and a 200 response is returned.

Once a user has registered, and hopefully verified their email, they will want to be able to change their password.

Changing passwords

A user will want to change their password, which requires a route that accepts their new password and their old password. The old password is checked to make the member's account more secure, as a malicious user gaining access via an unattended computer cannot change the member's password (without also knowing the member's password). The route will also need to check that the new password has sufficient complexity as with the registration route.

The route should also inform the user that the password has been changed by email. Doing so makes the member's account more secure as the member can take corrective action if they are informed about a password change that they didn't authorize. This email is defined by adding the following to *backend/src/backend/templates/password_changed.html*:

```
{% extends "email.html" %}

{% block content %}
  Your Tozo password has been successfully changed.
{% endblock %}
```

This route will update the password, which in a RESTful style means a PUT route on the member's password resource that returns 200 on success. It should return a 400 response if the password is not complex enough and a 401 response if the old password is incorrect. The following should be added to *backend/src/backend/blueprints/members.py*:

```
from typing import cast

from quart_auth import current_user, login_required
```

```python
from backend.models.member import select_member_by_id, update_
member_password

@dataclass
class PasswordData:
    current_password: str
    new_password: str

@blueprint.put("/members/password/")
@rate_limit(5, timedelta(minutes=1))
@login_required
@validate_request(PasswordData)
async def change_password(data: PasswordData) ->
ResponseReturnValue:
    """Update the members password.

    This allows the user to update their password.
    """
    strength = zxcvbn(data.new_password)
    if strength["score"] < MINIMUM_STRENGTH:
        raise APIError(400, "WEAK_PASSWORD")

    member_id = int(cast(str, current_user.auth_id))
    member = await select_member_by_id(
        g.connection, member_id
    )
    assert member is not None  # nosec
    passwords_match = bcrypt.checkpw(
        data.current_password.encode("utf-8"),
        member.password_hash.encode("utf-8"),
    )
    if not passwords_match:
        raise APIError(401, "INVALID_PASSWORD")

    hashed_password = bcrypt.hashpw(
        data.new_password.encode("utf-8"),
        bcrypt.gensalt(14),
```

```
    )
    await update_member_password(
        g.connection, member_id, hashed_password.decode()
    )
    await send_email(
        member.email,
        "Password changed",
        "password_changed.html",
        {},
    )
    return {}
```

As with the login route, this route has a lower rate limit to mitigate against brute force attacks. The code then checks the password strength before checking that the old password matches the hash stored in the database. If these checks pass, the password hash in the database is updated and an email is sent to the member.

This functionality is intentionally not useful for member's that have forgotten their password. In that case, they first need to request a password reset.

Requesting a password reset

If a member forgets their password, they'll want a way to reset it. This is typically provided by emailing the member a link that they can follow to a password reset page with the link containing a token to authorize the reset – as with the email verification. For this to work, we first need a route that accepts the user's email address and sends out the link. To start, let's add the following email content to *backend/ src/backend/templates/forgotten_password.html*:

```
{% extends "email.html" %}

{% block content %}
  You can use this
  <a href="{{ config['BASE_URL'] }}/reset-password/{{ token
    }}/">
    link
  </a>
  to reset your password.
{% endblock %}
```

The route itself should accept an email address, and in the RESTful style should be a PUT to the member email resource. The following should be added to *backend/src/backend/blueprints/members.py*:

```python
from pydantic import EmailStr

from backend.models.member import select_member_by_email

FORGOTTEN_PASSWORD_SALT = "forgotten password"  # nosec

@dataclass
class ForgottenPasswordData:
    email: EmailStr

@blueprint.put("/members/forgotten-password/")
@rate_limit(5, timedelta(minutes=1))
@validate_request(ForgottenPasswordData)
async def forgotten_password(data: ForgottenPasswordData) ->
ResponseReturnValue:
    """Call to trigger a forgotten password email.

    This requires a valid member email.
    """
    member = await select_member_by_email(
        g.connection, data.email
    )
    if member is not None:
        serializer = URLSafeTimedSerializer(
            current_app.secret_key,
            salt=FORGOTTEN_PASSWORD_SALT,
        )
        token = serializer.dumps(member.id)
        await send_email(
            member.email,
            "Forgotten password",
            "forgotten_password.html",
            {"token": token},
        )
    return {}
```

This route creates a token using the forgotten-password salt. It is important that the salt differs to ensure that these tokens cannot be used in place of the email verification token and vice versa. The token is then rendered into the email and sent to the member.

Resetting the password

If the member follows the link emailed out by the previous route, they will visit a page that allows them to enter a new password. Therefore, we need a route that accepts the new password and the token. This is achieved by adding the following to *backend/src/backend/blueprints/members.py*:

```python
ONE_DAY = int(timedelta(hours=24).total_seconds())


@dataclass
class ResetPasswordData:
    password: str
    token: str


@blueprint.put("/members/reset-password/")
@rate_limit(5, timedelta(minutes=1))
@validate_request(ResetPasswordData)
async def reset_password(data: ResetPasswordData) ->
ResponseReturnValue:
    """Call to reset a password using a token.

    This requires the user to supply a valid token and a
    new password.
    """
    serializer = URLSafeTimedSerializer(
        current_app.secret_key, salt=FORGOTTEN_PASSWORD_SALT
    )
    try:
        member_id = serializer.loads(data.token, max_age=ONE_
            DAY)
    except SignatureExpired:
        raise APIError(403, "TOKEN_EXPIRED")
    except BadSignature:
        raise APIError(400, "TOKEN_INVALID")
    else:
```

```
        strength = zxcvbn(data.password)
        if strength["score"] < MINIMUM_STRENGTH:
            raise APIError(400, "WEAK_PASSWORD")

        hashed_password = bcrypt.hashpw(
            data.password.encode("utf-8"),
            bcrypt.gensalt(14),
        )
        await update_member_password(
            g.connection, member_id, hashed_password.decode()
        )
        member = await select_member_by_id(
            g.connection, int(cast(str, current_user.auth_id))
        )
        assert member is not None  # nosec
        await send_email(
            member.email,
            "Password changed",
            "password_changed.html",
            {},
        )
    return {}
```

This route checks whether the token is valid, returning either a 400 if it is not or a 403 if it has expired. The expiry is important as it protects against a member's email being exposed in the future (as the token will have expired and hence is useless). Then, if the password is strong enough, the new hash is placed into the database.

Managing members

We've added functionality to create members and manage members' passwords. However, we haven't added functionality to manage a member's account itself, for example, to close and delete it. This functionality will be dependent on the regulatory rules of your app as, for example, you may be required to keep data for a certain length of time.

With this route, we have all the functionality we require for member accounts and can now focus on testing the functionality.

Testing the routes

We should test that these routes work as a user would expect. Firstly, let's test that new members can register and then log in by adding the following to *backend/tests/blueprints/test_members.py*:

```
import pytest
from quart import Quart


async def test_register(
    app: Quart, caplog: pytest.LogCaptureFixture
) -> None:
    test_client = app.test_client()
    data = {
        "email": "new@tozo.dev",
        "password": "testPassword2$",
    }
    await test_client.post("/members/", json=data)
    response = await test_client.post("/sessions/", json=data)
    assert response.status_code == 200
    assert "Sending welcome.html to new@tozo.dev" in caplog.
text
```

This test registers a new member with the email new@tozo.dev and then checks that the welcome email was sent to this address. Next, we need to check that the user can confirm their email address by adding the following to *backend/tests/blueprints/test_members.py*:

```
from itsdangerous import URLSafeTimedSerializer
from freezegun import freeze_time
from backend.blueprints.members import EMAIL_VERIFICATION_SALT


@pytest.mark.parametrize(
    "time, expected",
    [("2022-01-01", 403), (None, 200)],
)
async def test_verify_email(
    app: Quart, time: str | None, expected: int
) -> None:
    with freeze_time(time):
        signer = URLSafeTimedSerializer(
```

```
            app.secret_key, salt= EMAIL_VERIFICATION_SALT
        )
        token = signer.dumps(1)
    test_client = app.test_client()
    response = await test_client.put(
        "/members/email/", json={"token": token}
    )
    assert response.status_code == expected


async def test_verify_email_invalid_token(app: Quart) -> None:
    test_client = app.test_client()
    response = await test_client.put(
        "/members/email/", json={"token": "invalid"}
    )
    assert response.status_code == 400
```

The highlighted line allows us to ensure that expired tokens result in a 403 response while current tokens succeed. The second test ensures that invalid tokens result in a 400 response.

Next, we will test that members can change their password by adding the following to *backend/tests/blueprints/test_members.py*:

```
async def test_change_password(
    app: Quart, caplog: pytest.LogCaptureFixture
) -> None:
    test_client = app.test_client()
    data = {
        "email": "new_password@tozo.dev",
        "password": "testPassword2$",
    }
    response = await test_client.post("/members/", json=data)
    async with test_client.authenticated("2"):  # type: ignore
        response = await test_client.put(
            "/members/password/",
            json={
                "currentPassword": data["password"],
                "newPassword": "testPassword3$",
            }
```

```
    )
        assert response.status_code == 200
    assert "Sending password_changed.html to new@tozo.dev" in
caplog.text
```

This test registers a new member and then, while authenticated as that member, changes the password.

Then we can test that a user that has forgotten their password can request a reset link by adding the following to *backend/tests/blueprints/test_members.py*:

```
async def test_forgotten_password(
    app: Quart, caplog: pytest.LogCaptureFixture
) -> None:
    test_client = app.test_client()
    data = {"email": "member@tozo.dev"}
    response = await test_client.put(
        "/members/forgotten-password/", json=data
    )
    assert response.status_code == 200
    assert "Sending forgotten_password.html to member@tozo.dev"
in caplog.text
```

Now we have these simple tests in place, we can focus on the To-Do API.

Building the To-Do API

To manage to-dos, we need an API that provides functionality to create a new to-do, retrieve a to-do or to-dos, update a to-do, and delete a to-do (i.e., an API that has CRUD functionality). We'll do this by creating a to-do blueprint with a route per CRUD function.

CRUD functionality

CRUD stands for Create, Read, Update, and Delete, and is used to describe a set of functionalities. It is often used to describe the functionality of RESTful APIs. Typically, for a RESTful API, the Create route uses the POST HTTP method, Read uses GET, Update uses PUT, and Delete uses DELETE.

Creating the blueprint

The blueprint itself can be created with the following code in *backend/src/backend/blueprints/todos.py*:

```
from quart import Blueprint


blueprint = Blueprint("todos", __name__)
```

The blueprint then needs to be registered with the app, by adding the following to *backend/src/backend/run.py*:

```
from backend.blueprints.todos import blueprint as todos_
blueprint


app.register_blueprint(todos_blueprint)
```

With the blueprint created, we can now add specific functionality as routes.

Creating a to-do

The first functionality we need is to create a to-do. The route should expect the to-do data and return the complete to-do with a 201 status code on success. Returning the complete to-do is useful as it contains the to-do's ID and confirms that the data is added. A RESTful to-do creation route should use the POST verb and have a /todos/ path. The following should be added to *backend/src/backend/blueprints/todos.py*:

```
from dataclasses import dataclass
from datetime import datetime, timedelta
from typing import cast

from quart import g
from quart_auth import current_user, login_required
from quart_schema import validate_request, validate_response
from quart_rate_limiter import rate_limit

from backend.models.todo import insert_todo, Todo

@dataclass
class TodoData:
    complete: bool
```

```
    due: datetime | None
    task: str

@blueprint.post("/todos/")
@rate_limit(10, timedelta(seconds=10))
@login_required
@validate_request(TodoData)
@validate_response(Todo, 201)
async def post_todo(data: TodoData) -> tuple[Todo, int]:
    """Create a new Todo.

    This allows todos to be created and stored.
    """
    todo = await insert_todo(
        g.connection,
        int(cast(str, current_user.auth_id)),
        data.task,
        data.complete,
        data.due,
    )
    return todo, 201
```

The route is rate limited to prevent malicious usage, with the assumption that normal users are unlikely to create more than 10 to-dos in 10 seconds (1 a second on average). It is also a route that requires the user to be logged in. The final two decorators ensure that the request and response data represent the to-do data and a complete to-do.

The route function simply inserts the data into the database and returns the complete to-do. Next, users will need to read a to-do from the backend.

Reading a to-do

Users will need to read a to-do based on its ID. This will be implemented as a GET route with the ID specified in the path. The route should then either return the to-do or a 404 response if the to-do does not exist. The following should be added to *backend/src/backend/blueprints/todos.py*:

```
from backend.lib.api_error import APIError
from backend.models.todo import select_todo
```

```python
@blueprint.get("/todos/<int:id>/")
@rate_limit(10, timedelta(seconds=10))
@login_required
@validate_response(Todo)
async def get_todo(id: int) -> Todo:
    """Get a todo.

    Fetch a Todo by its ID.
    """
    todo = await select_todo(
        g.connection, id, int(cast(str, current_user.auth_id))
    )
    if todo is None:
        raise APIError(404, "NOT_FOUND")
    else:
        return todo
```

As with the creation route, this route includes rate limiting protection, requires the user to be logged in, and validates the response data. It then selects the to-do from the database based on the ID given in the path and returns it or a 404 response if no to-do exists. Note that the select_todo function requires the member's ID, ensuring that members cannot read other members' to-dos.

While reading a single to-do is useful, a user will also need to read all their to-dos in one call, which we'll add next.

Reading the to-dos

A user will need to read all their to-dos, which for a RESTFul API should use the GET verb and return a list of to-dos on success. We'll also allow the user to filter the to-dos based on the complete attribute, which should be optional and hence, in a RESTful API, is provided via a querystring. The querystring works via the request path, for example, /todos/?complete=true or /todos/?complete=false. The following should be added to *backend/src/backend/blueprints/todos.py*:

```python
from quart_schema import validate_querystring

from backend.models.todo import select_todos
```

```
@dataclass
class Todos:
    todos: list[Todo]


@dataclass
class TodoFilter:
    complete: bool | None = None


@blueprint.get("/todos/")
@rate_limit(10, timedelta(seconds=10))
@login_required
@validate_response(Todos)
@validate_querystring(TodoFilter)
async def get_todos(query_args: TodoFilter) -> Todos:
    """Get the todos.

    Fetch all the Todos optionally based on the
    complete status.
    """
    todos = await select_todos(
        g.connection,
        int(cast(str, current_user.auth_id)),
        query_args.complete,
    )
    return Todos(todos=todos)
```

This route includes rate limit protection, requires logged-in usage, validates the response data, and includes validation of the `querystring` parameters. We can now move on to allowing updates to a to-do.

Updating a to-do

We need to provide functionality for members to update the data that makes up a to-do. For a RESTFul API, this route should use the PUT verb, expect the to-do data, and return the complete to-do on success or a 404 if the to-do does not exist. The following should be added to *backend/src/backend/blueprints/todos.py*:

```
from backend.models.todo import update_todo
```

```
@blueprint.put("/todos/<int:id>/")
@rate_limit(10, timedelta(seconds=10))
@login_required
@validate_request(TodoData)
@validate_response(Todo)
async def put_todo(id: int, data: TodoData) -> Todo:
    """Update the identified todo

    This allows the todo to be replaced with the request data.
    """
    todo = await update_todo(
        g.connection,
        id,
        int(cast(str, current_user.auth_id)),
        data.task,
        data.complete,
        data.due,
    )
    if todo is None:
        raise APIError(404, "NOT_FOUND")
    else:
        return todo
```

This route includes rate limit protection, requires logged-in usage, and validates the request and response data. It then updates the to-do and returns the updated to-do or a 404 response if there is no to-do for the provided ID. Next, we'll allow users to delete to-dos.

Deleting a to-do

For a RESTFul API, the to-do deletion route should use the DELETE verb, and return 202 whether the to-do exists or not. The following should be added to *backend/src/backend/blueprints/todos.py*:

```
from quart import ResponseReturnValue

from backend.models.todo import delete_todo

@blueprint.delete("/todos/<int:id>/")
@rate_limit(10, timedelta(seconds=10))
```

```
@login_required
async def todo_delete(id: int) -> ResponseReturnValue:
    """Delete the identified todo

    This will delete the todo.
    """
    await delete_todo(
        g.connection, id, int(cast(str, current_user.auth_id))
    )
    return "", 202
```

This route includes rate limit protection, requires logged-in usage, and deletes the to-do with the given ID as long as it belongs to the logged-in member.

With all the functionality for to-dos in place, we can now focus on testing that it works correctly.

Testing the routes

We should test that these routes work as a user would expect. Firstly, we need to ensure we can create new to-dos by adding the following to *backend/tests/blueprints/test_todos.py*:

```
from quart import Quart

async def test_post_todo(app: Quart) -> None:
    test_client = app.test_client()
    async with test_client.authenticated("1"):  # type: ignore
        response = await test_client.post(
            "/todos/",
            json={
                "complete": False, "due": None, "task": "Test
                    task"
            },
        )
        assert response.status_code == 201
        assert (await response.get_json())["id"] > 0
```

Next, we can ensure we can read to-dos by adding the following to *backend/tests/blueprints/test_todos.py*:

```
async def test_get_todo(app: Quart) -> None:
    test_client = app.test_client()
```

```
    async with test_client.authenticated("1"):  # type: ignore
        response = await test_client.get("/todos/1/")
        assert response.status_code == 200
        assert (await response.get_json())["task"] == "Test
            Task"
```

Continuing along the CRUD functionality, we can ensure that to-dos can be updated by adding the following to *backend/tests/blueprints/test_todos.py*:

```
async def test_put_todo(app: Quart) -> None:
    test_client = app.test_client()
    async with test_client.authenticated("1"):  # type: ignore
        response = await test_client.post(
            "/todos/",
            json={
                "complete": False, "due": None, "task": "Test
                    task"
            },
        )
        todo_id = (await response.get_json())["id"]

        response = await test_client.put(
            f"/todos/{todo_id}/",
            json={
                "complete": False, "due": None, "task":
                    "Updated"
            },
        )
        assert (await response.get_json())["task"] == "Updated"

        response = await test_client.get(f"/todos/{todo_id}/")
        assert (await response.get_json())["task"] == "Updated"
```

Finally, we can ensure that to-dos can be deleted by adding the following to *backend/tests/blueprints/test_todos.py*:

```
async def test_delete_todo(app: Quart) -> None:
    test_client = app.test_client()
    async with test_client.authenticated("1"):  # type: ignore
```

```
response = await test_client.post(
    "/todos/",
    json={
        "complete": False, "due": None, "task": "Test
            task"
    },
)
todo_id = (await response.get_json())["id"]

await test_client.delete(f"/todos/{todo_id}/")

response = await test_client.get(f"/todos/{todo_id}/")
assert response.status_code == 404
```

With these tests, we have all the functionality we need to manage to-dos.

Summary

In this chapter, we've defined how we are storing the data in the database and then built an API to manage sessions, members, and to-dos. This includes all the functionality our app will need via an easy-to-understand RESTful API.

While the to-do functionality is unlikely to be directly useful to your app, the CRUD functionality is a pattern you should use. In addition, the member and session APIs could be used directly in your app. Finally, you've hopefully gained an understanding of what makes a good RESTful API that you can apply and use elsewhere.

In the next chapter, we'll create a styled frontend, including validated data entry in React, that we can use with this API or any other.

Further reading

We've built a fairly simple RESTful API in this chapter. As your API's complexity increases, I'd recommend following the best practices at `https://www.vinaysahni.com/best-practices-for-a-pragmatic-restful-api`.

4

Creating a Reusable Frontend with React

In the previous chapter, we built an API to manage sessions, members, and to-dos. In this chapter, we will create a frontend that is capable of connecting to that API or any other you may wish to use. In addition, we'll add styling, routing, validated data entry, and feedback via toasts.

Styling, routing, data entry, and feedback are all features that will be useful in your app and are not specific to to-dos. Therefore, at the end of this chapter, we'll have created a frontend to which we can add a user interface with any specific functionality.

So, in this chapter, we will cover the following topics:

- Enhancing the basic React app
- Adding routing
- Enabling data entry
- Managing the app state
- Supporting toast feedback

Technical requirements

The following additional folders are required in this chapter and should be created:

```
tozo
└── frontend
    └── src
        └── components
```

To follow the development in this chapter using the companion repository, `https://github.com/pgjones/tozo`, see the commits between the `r1-ch4-start` and `r1-ch4-end` tags.

Enhancing the basic React app

In the *Installing NodeJS for frontend development* section of *Chapter 1, Setting Up Our System for Development*, we used the `create-react-app` tool to create a standard React app, which we can now configure for our usage.

First, as we are using a frontend development server, we will need to proxy API requests to our backend by adding the following to *frontend/package.json*:

```
{
  ...,
  "proxy": "http://localhost:5050"
}
```

The highlighted ellipsis represents the existing code; note the additional trailing comma that has been added.

Next, we'll configure the import system so that we can use full paths with *src* as the root (i.e., *src/components/Component*) rather than, for example, *../components/Component*. This makes the imported file easier to find as we can always relate the path to the *src* directory. It also matches the type of import paths we've used already in the backend. To do so, we need to add the following to *frontend/tsconfig.json*:

```
{
  "compilerOptions": {
    "baseUrl": "./",
    ...
  }
}
```

The `compilerOptions` section should already exist, to which the `baseUrl` entry should be added (the highlighted ellipsis represents the existing code). In addition, we need to install `eslint-import-resolver-typescript` to inform `eslint` to use the same `baseUrl` by running the following in the *frontend* directory:

```
npm install --save-dev eslint-import-resolver-typescript
```

This is then configured by adding the following to the `eslintConfig` section in *frontend/package.json*:

```
"eslintConfig": {
  "extends": [...],
  "settings": {
    "import/resolver": {
      "typescript": {}
    }
  }
}
```

The highlighted line represents the existing code within the existing `eslintConfig` section.

With these small configuration changes, we can now focus on styling the app, adding page titles, and adding an authentication context.

Styling the app

It takes a lot of effort to build a design system and use it consistently to style an app. Fortunately, MUI (`mui.com`) is an existing React component library that can be used to create apps using the Material Design System pioneered by Google. MUI is installed by running the following in the *frontend* directory:

```
npm install @mui/material @mui/icons-material @mui/lab
@emotion/react @emotion/styled
```

As material design and MUI are based on the Roboto font, we will need to install that as well by running the following in the *frontend* directory:

```
npm install @fontsource/roboto
```

This font also needs to be included in the bundle and hence the following imports should be added to *frontend/src/App.tsx*:

```
import "@fontsource/roboto/300.css";
import "@fontsource/roboto/400.css";
import "@fontsource/roboto/500.css";
import "@fontsource/roboto/700.css";
```

The number refers to the font weight (boldness); by default, MUI only uses 300, 400, 500, and 700 weights, so these are the only ones we need.

> **Semantic HTML**
>
> MUI is very good at using the most descriptive HTML tags for the elements; for example, MUI buttons use the Button tag rather than styling a div tag. This is called **semantic HTML** as it uses HTML to reinforce the semantics of the content. This is an important thing to do as it aids accessibility and improves the user experience.

So far, our app will look exactly the same as the default MUI app, but we can change that by theming our app. To do so, let's create a ThemeProvider element by placing the following in *frontend/src/ThemeProvider.tsx*:

```tsx
import { useMemo } from "react";
import { PaletteMode } from "@mui/material";
import CssBaseline from "@mui/material/CssBaseline";
import useMediaQuery from "@mui/material/useMediaQuery";
import { createTheme, ThemeProvider as MuiThemeProvider } from
"@mui/material/styles";

interface IProps {
  children: React.ReactNode;
}

const ThemeProvider = ({ children }: IProps) => {
  const prefersDarkMode = useMediaQuery("(prefers-color-scheme:
    dark)");
  const theme = useMemo(
    () => {
      const palette = {
        mode: (prefersDarkMode ? "dark" : "light") as
          PaletteMode,
      };
      return createTheme({ palette });
    },
    [prefersDarkMode]
  );

  return (
    <MuiThemeProvider theme={theme}>
      <CssBaseline enableColorScheme />
```

```
      { children }
    </MuiThemeProvider>
  );
};
```

```
export default ThemeProvider;
```

Here, we've used the `CssBaseline` component to reset and normalize the browser's styling, thereby ensuring our app looks the same in all browsers. We've also used the `prefers-color-scheme` system preference to switch the app to a dark mode if the user's system indicates that's their preference.

The `ThemeProvider` should be rendered in the `App` component as the parent of any styled components, i.e. *frontend/src/App.tsx* should be as follows:

```
import ThemeProvider from "src/ThemeProvider";
const App = () => {
  return (
    <ThemeProvider>
    </ThemeProvider>
  );
}
```

Note that I've changed the `App` function definition syntax to use the arrow function syntax rather than the function definition syntax as created for us by `create-react-app`.

Function style

TypeScript allows for functions to be defined with a `function` keyword or via the arrow `=>` syntax. While there are differences between these two styles, for a React component it makes no practical difference which style is used. In this book, I'll use the arrow syntax based on my preference.

As we've changed the `App` component, we also need to update the test by replacing *frontend/src/App.test.tsx* with the following:

```
import React from "react";
import { render } from "@testing-library/react";
import App from "./App";
```

```
test("renders the app", () => {
  render(<App />);
});
```

We are aiming for our app to be usable on small mobile screens, large desktop screens, and everything in-between. We can achieve this by building the app for small mobile screens and allowing it to resize with the screen size. However, as you can see in *Figure 4.1*, this starts to look odd with large horizontal widths:

Figure 4.1: How the app would look without a Container

This is fixed by adding a `Container` within the `ThemeProvider` in *frontend/src/App.tsx*:

```
import Container from "@mui/material/Container";
const App = () => {
  return (
    <ThemeProvider>
      <Container maxWidth="md">
      </Container>
    </ThemeProvider>
  );
}
```

The highlighted lines show the additions, and the result is shown in *Figure 4.2*:

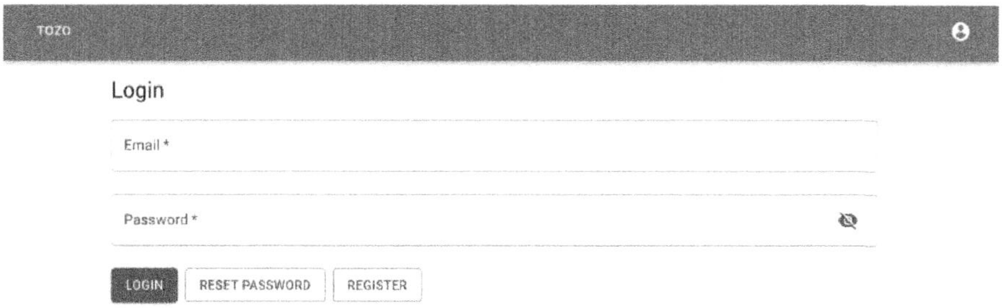

Figure 4.2: How the app looks with the Container

With the styling in place, we can now add a title for each page.

Adding page titles

We can give the user a better experience by configuring the page title as it is displayed in the user's browser, as seen in *Figure 4.3*:

Figure 4.3: The title (as displayed by Chrome)

To set the title, we can use `react-helmet-async`, which is installed by running the following in the *frontend* directory:

```
npm install react-helmet-async
```

To use `react-helmet-async`, we need to add `HelmetProvider` as an ancestor to our components by adding the following to *frontend/src/App.tsx*:

```
import { Helmet, HelmetProvider } from "react-helmet-async";
const App = () => {
  return (
    <HelmetProvider>
      <Helmet>
        <title>Tozo</title>
      </Helmet>
      <ThemeProvider>
        <Container maxWidth="md">
```

```
        </Container>
      </ThemeProvider>
    </HelmetProvider>
  );
}
```

The highlighted lines will set the default page title to be Tozo and should be added to the existing code.

We can now create a Title component that both sets the title displayed by the browser and displays clear title text on the page, by adding the following to *frontend/src/components/Title.tsx*:

```
import Typography from "@mui/material/Typography";
import { Helmet } from "react-helmet-async";

interface IProps {
  title: string;
}

const Title = ({ title }: IProps) => (
  <>
    <Helmet>
      <title>Tozo | {title}</title>
    </Helmet>
    <Typography component="h1" variant="h5">{title}
    </Typography>
  </>
);


export default Title;
```

With this small addition, we can now consider how the app knows whether the user is authenticated or not.

Adding an authentication context

The frontend app will need to track whether the user is currently authenticated (logged in) and show the login or registration page if they are not. This is something that will be useful throughout the app and hence we'll use a React context, specifically called `AuthContext`, by adding the following to *frontend/src/AuthContext.tsx*:

```
import { createContext, useState } from "react";

interface IAuth {
  authenticated: boolean;
  setAuthenticated: (value: boolean) => void;
}

export const AuthContext = createContext<IAuth>({
  authenticated: true,
  setAuthenticated: (value: boolean) => {},
});

interface IProps {
  children?: React.ReactNode;
}

export const AuthContextProvider = ({ children }: IProps) => {
  const [authenticated, setAuthenticated] = useState(true);

  return (
    <AuthContext.Provider
      value={{ authenticated, setAuthenticated }}
    >
      {children}
    </AuthContext.Provider>
  );
};
```

> **React context and prop drilling**
>
> React context is best used to share things globally within a React component tree. This is because any descendant of the provider will be able to access the context. We could also achieve this by passing the context via props through the tree, called prop drilling. However, prop drilling soon becomes cumbersome when there are many components to pass through.

To make this context available throughout the app, we can add the provider to *frontend/src/App.tsx*:

```
import { AuthContextProvider } from "src/AuthContext";

const App = () => {
  return (
    <AuthContextProvider>
      <HelmetProvider>
        <Helmet>
          <title>Tozo</title>
        </Helmet>
        <ThemeProvider>
          <Container maxWidth="md">
          </Container>
        </ThemeProvider>
      </HelmetProvider>
    </AuthContextProvider>
  );
}
```

The highlighted lines should be added to the existing code.

This then allows the authentication state to be accessed in any component via a `useContext` hook:

```
import { AuthContext } from "src/AuthContext";

const { authenticated } = React.useContext(AuthContext);
```

We'll make use of this context next, as we set up the routing.

Adding routing

Frontend apps are usually made up of multiple pages, as is our to-do app. We will achieve this with routing, which allows different page components to render, depending on the app's path. As we are building a single-page app, this routing will be done in the frontend code, rather than the backend, which would be the case for a multi-page app.

We'll use React Router (`reactrouter.com`) to handle routing in our app. It is installed by running the following command in the *frontend* directory:

```
npm install react-router-dom
```

> **Single-page app**
>
> A **single-page app**, often called an **SPA**, refers to a web app whereby only a single page is fetched from the backend server. This single page is then able to render all the pages within the app. This is an advantage as navigating from one page to another is typically quicker in an SPA; however, this comes with the cost of a larger initial download.

I find it clearer to place all the routing into a single component called `Router`, with each page being an individual `Route`. The `Router` is defined by adding the following to *frontend/src/Router.tsx*:

```
import { BrowserRouter, Routes } from "react-router-dom";

const Router = () => (
  <BrowserRouter>
    <Routes>
      {/* Place routes here */}
    </Routes>
  </BrowserRouter>
);


export default Router;
```

The `Router` component should then be rendered within the `Container` component as shown by the following, which should be added to *frontend/src/App.tsx*:

```
import Router from "src/Router";

const App = () => {
  return (
    <AuthContextProvider>
      <HelmetProvider>
        <Helmet>
          <title>Tozo</title>
```

```
        </Helmet>
        <ThemeProvider>
          <Container maxWidth="md">
            <Router />
          </Container>
        </ThemeProvider>
      </HelmetProvider>
    </AuthContextProvider>
  );
}
```

The highlighted lines should be added to the existing code.

We can now add authentication to our routing to ensure that some of the pages only render for a logged-in user.

Requiring authentication

A significant fraction of the routes in the app should only be available for users who are logged in. Therefore, we need a component that checks whether the user is authenticated and renders the page. Alternatively, if the user isn't authenticated, the app redirects the user to the login page. This is done by creating the following component in *frontend/src/components/RequireAuth.tsx*:

```
import { useContext } from "react";
import { Navigate, useLocation } from "react-router-dom";

import { AuthContext } from "src/AuthContext";

interface IProps {
  children: React.ReactNode;
}

const RequireAuth = ({ children }: IProps) => {
  const { authenticated } = useContext(AuthContext);
  const location = useLocation();

  if (authenticated) {
    return <>{children}</>;
  } else {
```

```
      return <Navigate state={{ from: location }} to="/login/"
/>;
  }
};
```

```
export default RequireAuth;
```

The navigation state is set to include the current location so that the user can be redirected back to the page after successfully authenticating.

We can then use `RequireAuth` as a wrapper around a `Page` component within a `Route`, as this ensures that the `Page` only renders if the user is authenticated, for example (this shouldn't be added to our app):

```
<Route
  element={<RequireAuth><Page /></RequireAuth>}
  path= "/private/"
/>
```

The final aspect of the routing setup is to control the scrolling when navigating.

Resetting scrolling on navigation

When a user navigates and changes the page in the app, they will expect to view the new page from the start (i.e., the top of the page). As the view, or scroll position, will remain fixed on a React Router navigation, we will need to reset it to the top ourselves. We can do this We can do this by scrolling up to the window top on a change in the path via the following component, as placed in *frontend/src/ components/ScrollToTop.tsx*:

```
import { useEffect } from "react";
import { useLocation } from "react-router";

const ScrollToTop = () => {
  const { pathname } = useLocation();

  useEffect(() => {
    window.scrollTo(0, 0);
  }, [pathname]);

  return null;
```

```
};
```

```
export default ScrollToTop;
```

The `useEffect` will only trigger when its `pathname` dependency changes, hence the scrolling only occurs on navigation.

This component should be rendered within `BrowserRouter` in the `Router` component by adding the following to *frontend/src/Router.tsx*:

```
import ScrollToTop from "src/components/ScrollToTop";

const Router = () => (
  <BrowserRouter>
    <ScrollToTop />
    <Routes>
      {/* Place routes here */}
    </Routes>
  </BrowserRouter>
);
```

The highlighted lines should be added to the existing code.

In order for the frontend tests to pass, we will need to define the `window.scrollTo` function by adding the following to *frontend/src/setupTests.ts*:

```
window.scrollTo = (x, y) => {
  document.documentElement.scrollTop = y;
}
```

This is all we require to enable pages via routing in our app; now, we can focus on how the user will enter data.

Enabling data entry

Users of our app will need to enter their email and password to log in, and then a description, due date, and completion for their to-do tasks. These fields will need to be grouped into forms; building forms with a good user experience takes a lot of effort as the form must be validated and the touched state, error state, and focused state must be managed for each field and the form itself.

> **Form input states**
>
> A form input box will need to display a variety of different states to help the user understand how it is used and when there is an issue. To start, the input will be in an empty state with no value and no error. This is important as the input should not show an error until the user touches/interacts with it. Then, while the user is interacting with it, the input should show that it is focused. Finally, after the input has been touched, if the value doesn't validate, it needs to show an error state.

We'll use Formik (`formik.org`) to manage the form and field states and Yup (`github.com/jquense/yup`) to validate the inputted data. These are installed by running the following in the *frontend* directory:

```
npm install formik yup
```

As we will use MUI for styling and Formik to manage the state, we will need to create field components that combine the two. While this will differ for each field, the following function is useful to all the components and should be placed in *frontend/src/utils.tsx*:

```
import { FieldMetaProps } from "formik";
import React from "react";

export const combineHelperText = <T, >(
    helperText: React.ReactNode | string | undefined,
    meta: FieldMetaProps<T>,
) => {
  if (Boolean(meta.error) && meta.touched) {
    if (typeof helperText === "string") {
      return `${meta.error}. ${helperText ?? ""}`;
    } else {
      return (<>{meta.error}. {helperText}</>);
    }
  } else {
    return helperText;
  }
}
```

This generic function works by extracting the error from the Formik meta props and displaying it alongside the helper text if there is an error and the user has touched the input. The comma in `<T, >` is required to distinguish between the generic usage we desire and what a `<T>` JSX element alone implies.

With Formik installed and the helper function ready to use, we can start creating the field components, beginning with a checkbox field.

Implementing a styled checkbox field

In our app, we'll need a checkbox field to indicate whether a to-do is complete or to indicate whether the user wants to be remembered when logging in. The following should be added to *frontend/src/components/CheckboxField.tsx*:

```
import Checkbox from "@mui/material/Checkbox";
import FormControl from "@mui/material/FormControl";
import FormControlLabel from "@mui/material/FormControlLabel";
import FormHelperText from "@mui/material/FormHelperText";
import { FieldHookConfig, useField } from "formik";

import { combineHelperText } from "src/utils";

type IProps = FieldHookConfig<boolean> & {
  fullWidth?: boolean;
  helperText?: string;
  label: string;
  required?: boolean;
};

const CheckboxField = (props: IProps) => {
  const [field, meta] = useField<boolean>(props);

  return (
    <FormControl
      component="fieldset"
      error={Boolean(meta.error) && meta.touched}
      fullWidth={props.fullWidth}
      margin="normal"
      required={props.required}
    >
      <FormControlLabel
        control={<Checkbox {...field} checked={field.value} />}
        label={props.label}
```

```
      />
      <FormHelperText>
        {combineHelperText(props.helperText, meta)}
      </FormHelperText>
    </FormControl>
  );
};

export default CheckboxField;
```

While most of this code is to style a checkbox as specified in the material design system, the key aspect is the usage of the `useField` hook to extract the Formik state for usage in the MUI components.

We can now move on to the next field, for date entry.

Implementing a styled date field

We'll need a date field for the user to specify a due date for a to-do, which will look like *Figure 4.4*:

Figure 4.4: The date picker on a mobile screen

To do so, we'll make use of a MUI-X (mui.com/x) component rather than the inbuilt browser date picker, as the MUI-X picker is much easier for users to use. MUI-X is a set of advanced MUI components and hence works with, and follows, the same styling as MUI. Alongside MUI-X, we also need date-fns to parse strings into the Date instances.

Both are installed by running the following in the *frontend* folder:

```
npm install @mui/x-date-pickers date-fns
```

With these libraries installed, we can create a DateField component that provides a date picker as seen in *Figure 4.4* by adding the following to *frontend/src/components/DateField.tsx*:

```
import TextField, { TextFieldProps } from "@mui/material/
TextField";
import { AdapterDateFns } from "@mui/x-date-pickers/
AdapterDateFns";
import { DatePicker } from "@mui/x-date-pickers/DatePicker";
import { LocalizationProvider } from "@mui/x-date-pickers/
LocalizationProvider";
import { FieldHookConfig, useField } from "formik";

import { combineHelperText } from "src/utils";

const DateField = (
  props: FieldHookConfig<Date | null> & TextFieldProps
) => {
  const [field, meta, helpers] = useField<Date | null>(props);

  return (
    <LocalizationProvider dateAdapter={AdapterDateFns}>
      <DatePicker
        label={props.label}
        value={field.value}
        onChange={(newValue) => helpers.setValue(newValue)}
        renderInput={(params) => (
          <TextField
            fullWidth={props.fullWidth}
            {...params}
            helperText={combineHelperText(props.helperText,
```

```
meta)}
            />
        )}
      />
    </LocalizationProvider>
  );
};


export default DateField;
```

Next, we can add a field component for entering emails.

Implementing a styled email field

We'll need an email field for the user to log in and register. To do so, the following should be added to *frontend/src/components/EmailField.tsx*:

```
import TextField, { TextFieldProps } from "@mui/material/
TextField";
import { FieldHookConfig, useField } from "formik";

import { combineHelperText } from "src/utils";

const EmailField = (props: FieldHookConfig<string> &
TextFieldProps) => {
  const [field, meta] = useField<string>(props);

  return (
    <TextField
      {...props}
      autoComplete="email"
      error={Boolean(meta.error) && meta.touched}
      helperText={combineHelperText(props.helperText, meta)}
      margin="normal"
      type="email"
      {...field}
    />
  );
```

```
};


export default EmailField;
```

Next, we can add a simple text field.

Implementing a styled text field

We'll need a text field for the user to enter the to-do task information. To do so, the following should be added to *frontend/src/components/TextField.tsx*:

```
import MUITextField, { TextFieldProps } from "@mui/material/
TextField";
import { FieldHookConfig, useField } from "formik";


import { combineHelperText } from "src/utils";

const TextField = (props: FieldHookConfig<string> &
TextFieldProps) => {
  const [field, meta] = useField<string>(props);

  return (
    <MUITextField
      {...props}
      error={Boolean(meta.error) && meta.touched}
      helperText={combineHelperText(props.helperText, meta)}
      margin="normal"
      type="text"
      {...field}
    />
  );
};


export default TextField;
```

Finally, we can add a password entry field.

Implementing a styled password field

We'll need a password field for the user to enter their existing password when logging in or changing their password. This field should have a visibility toggle button that makes the password visible, as this helps the user get their password correct.

To do this, the following should be added to *frontend/src/components/PasswordField.tsx*:

```
import IconButton from "@mui/material/IconButton";
import InputAdornment from "@mui/material/InputAdornment";
import TextField, { TextFieldProps } from "@mui/material/
TextField";
import Visibility from "@mui/icons-material/Visibility";
import VisibilityOff from "@mui/icons-material/VisibilityOff";
import { FieldHookConfig, useField } from "formik";
import { useState } from "react";

import { combineHelperText } from "src/utils";

const PasswordField = (props: FieldHookConfig<string> &
TextFieldProps) => {
  const [field, meta] = useField<string>(props);
  const [showPassword, setShowPassword] = useState(false);

  return (
    <TextField
      {...props}
      InputProps={{
        endAdornment: (
          <InputAdornment position="end">
            <IconButton
              onClick={() => setShowPassword((value) =>
                !value)}
              tabIndex={-1}
            >
              {showPassword ? <Visibility /> :
                <VisibilityOff />}
            </IconButton>
          </InputAdornment>
```

```
      ),
    }}
    error={Boolean(meta.error) && meta.touched}
    helperText={combineHelperText(props.helperText, meta)}
    margin="normal"
    type={showPassword ? "text" : "password"}
    {...field}
  />
  );
};


export default PasswordField;
```

The visibility button is given a `tabIndex` value of −1 to take it out of the tab flow, so that pressing the *Tab* key after entering the password takes the focus to the next field and not the visibility button, thereby matching the user's expectations.

Implementing a styled password strength field

The existing password field allows users to enter a password but gives them no indication of how strong the password is. This is something that will be useful when the user is registering or changing their password. In the past, apps would mandate that special uppercase and lowercase characters should be present for a strong password. Yet this, sadly, leads to weaker passwords. So instead, we will require the password to be strong enough by calculating its entropy (this is something we already did in *Chapter 2, Creating a Reusable Backend with Quart*).

Only checking the strength in the backend API call leads to a poor user experience as it takes too long for the user to receive feedback on the strength of their password. Fortunately, there is a `zxcvbn` version that we can use to provide users instant feedback on the strength of their password in the frontend.

To start, we should install it by running the following in the *frontend* directory:

```
npm install zxcvbn
npm install --save-dev @types/zxcvbn
```

We'll want this field to give immediate visual feedback to the user on the strength of their password, both as a color that turns more green as the password strength improves, and as text that says **Good** or **Strong** as appropriate. So, let's add the following function to *frontend/src/components/PasswordWithStrengthField.tsx*:

```
const scoreToDisplay = (score: number) => {
  let progressColor = "other.red";
```

```
  let helperText = "Weak";

  switch (score) {
    case 25:
      progressColor = "other.pink";
      break;
    case 50:
      progressColor = "other.orange";
      break;
    case 75:
      progressColor = "other.yellow";
      helperText = "Good";
      break;
    case 100:
      progressColor = "other.green";
      helperText = "Strong";
      break;
  }
  return [progressColor, helperText];
};
```

We can then use this function in the field itself by adding the following to *frontend/src/components/ PasswordWithStrengthField.tsx*:

```
import LinearProgress from "@mui/material/LinearProgress";
import { TextFieldProps } from "@mui/material/TextField";
import { FieldHookConfig, useField } from "formik";
import zxcvbn from "zxcvbn";

import PasswordField from "src/components/PasswordField";

const PasswordWithStrengthField = (
  props: FieldHookConfig<string> & TextFieldProps,
) => {
  const [field] = useField<string>(props);
  const result = zxcvbn(field.value ?? "");
  const score = (result.score * 100) / 4;
```

```
const [progressColor, helperText] = scoreToDisplay(score);

return (
  <>
    <PasswordField {...props} helperText={helperText} />
    <LinearProgress
      sx={{
        "& .MuiLinearProgress-barColorPrimary": {
          backgroundColor: progressColor,
        },
        backgroundColor: "action.selected",
        margin: "0 4px 24px 4px",
      }}
      value={score}
      variant="determinate"
    />
  </>
);
};


export default PasswordWithStrengthField;
```

This code renders a `LinearProgress` component below the existing `PasswordField` and colors it based on the `scoreToDisplay` function already added.

The `PasswordWithStrengthField` uses zxcvbn to determine the strength of the password. This means that any component that directly imports `PasswordWithStrengthField` will add zxcvbn to the bundle it is in, which is a problem, as zxcvbn is very large. Therefore, to only load zxcvbn when required, we can use React's lazy loading and suspense system by adding the following to *frontend/src/components/LazyPasswordWithStrengthField.tsx*:

```
import { TextFieldProps } from "@mui/material/TextField";
import { lazy, Suspense } from "react";
import { FieldHookConfig } from "formik";


import PasswordField from "src/components/PasswordField";
```

```
const PasswordWithStrengthField = lazy(
  () => import("src/components/PasswordWithStrengthField"),
);


const LazyPasswordWithStrengthField = (
  props: FieldHookConfig<string> & TextFieldProps,
) => (
  <Suspense fallback={<PasswordField {...props} />}>
    <PasswordWithStrengthField {...props} />
  </Suspense>
);


export default LazyPasswordWithStrengthField;
```

Now the `PasswordField` will be shown to the user until zxcvbn has been downloaded, thereby improving the user experience by ensuring it is only downloaded if the user needs it.

These are all the custom fields we need for our to-do app; next, we need a set of styled action buttons.

Implementing styled form actions

The fields we've implemented will be contained in forms that will need to be submitted. Therefore, let's add a useful helper `FormActions` component that allows the user to submit the form as the primary action or to navigate elsewhere instead as secondary actions. The code for this follows and should be added to *frontend/src/components/FormActions.tsx*:

```
import Button from "@mui/material/Button";
import LoadingButton from "@mui/lab/LoadingButton";
import Stack from "@mui/material/Stack";
import { Link } from "react-router-dom";

interface ILink {
  label: string;
  to: string;
  state?: any;
}

interface IProps {
  disabled: boolean;
```

```
  isSubmitting: boolean;
  label: string;
  links?: ILink[];
}

const FormActions = ({ disabled, isSubmitting, label, links }:
IProps) => (
  <Stack direction="row" spacing={1} sx={{ marginTop: 2 }}>
    <LoadingButton
      disabled={disabled}
      loading={isSubmitting}
      type="submit"
      variant="contained"
    >
      {label}
    </LoadingButton>
    {(links ?? []).map(({ label, to, state }) => (
      <Button
        component={Link}
        key={to}
        state={state}
        to={to}
        variant="outlined"
      >
        {label}
      </Button>
    ))}
  </Stack>
);

export default FormActions;
```

The primary action is displayed using a LoadingButton component as it allows us to indicate to the user that the form submission is in progress via a spinning circle. Without this feedback, the user may think the app has frozen or ignored their click.

We now have all the fields and helper components we need for users to enter data. This means we can focus on how we will manage the app's state and particularly how data is fetched from the backend and stored in the app's state.

Managing the app state

As with the backend, it helps to have models that represent the data used in the app. These models will validate the data, help the linters ensure that we are using the data correctly, and ensure that the correct types are used. We will also use the model to correctly convert to and from the JSON representation used to communicate with the backend API.

The to-do model needs to be constructed from JSON, based on what is received from the backend or from data that the user entered. Then, the model needs to output as JSON so that this output can be sent to the backend. In addition, the model should validate that the data it is constructed from is of the correct structure and convert types (i.e., from strings representing dates in JSON to Date instances).

We only need a model for to-dos in the frontend, and hence we need the following in *frontend/src/ models.ts*:

```
import { formatISO } from "date-fns";
import * as yup from "yup";

const todoSchema = yup.object({
  complete: yup.boolean().required(),
  due: yup.date().nullable(),
  id: yup.number().required().positive().integer(),
  task: yup.string().trim().min(1).defined().strict(true),
});

export class Todo {
  complete: boolean;
  due: Date | null;
  id: number;
  task: string;

  constructor(data: any) {
    const validatedData = todoSchema.validateSync(data);
    this.complete = validatedData.complete;
    this.due = validatedData.due ?? null;
    this.id = validatedData.id;
```

```
      this.task = validatedData.task;
  }

  toJSON(): any {
    return {
      complete: this.complete,
      due:
        this.due !== null
          ? formatISO(this.due, { representation: "date" })
          : null,
      id: this.id,
      task: this.task,
    };
  }
}
```

The todoSchema is used in the constructor to confirm the data is of the correct structure and to convert the types. The toJSON method is a standard JavaScript method to convert objects to JSON-compatible structures, which is done by converting the due date to an ISO 8601 formatted string.

While this model is specific to our app, using a class with yup validation is a good pattern for any app's data.

With a model in place, we can now communicate with the backend, which we'll focus on next.

Communicating with the backend

We'll need to send and receive data from the backend API and then store it in the local state for usage in the various components that will render it. To begin, let's install axios as it has a nicer API for sending and receiving JSON than the inbuilt fetch function. It is installed by running the following in the *frontend* folder:

```
npm install axios
```

We will need to store the data received in a way that allows it to be used across multiple components. To manage this state, we'll use React-Query (https://tanstack.com/query/v4), as it is pleasant and easy to use. To start, let's install it by running the following in the *frontend* directory:

```
npm install @tanstack/react-query
```

To use React-Query, a QueryClient must be provided via React-Query's QueryClientProvider. This is achieved by adding the following to *frontend/src/App.tsx*:

```
import { QueryClient, QueryClientProvider } from "@tanstack/
react-query";

const queryClient = new QueryClient();

const App => {
  return (
    <QueryClientProvider client={queryClient}>
      <AuthContextProvider>
        <HelmetProvider>
          <Helmet>
            <title>Tozo</title>
          </Helmet>
          <ThemeProvider>
            <Container maxWidth="md">
              <Router />
            </Container>
          </ThemeProvider>
        </HelmetProvider>
      </AuthContextProvider>
    </QueryClientProvider>
  );
};
```

The highlighted lines should be added to the existing code.

We need to adapt React-Query so that requests that aren't authenticated result in changes to the AuthContext. This is to handle cases where a user visits a page without logging in first. We'll also only allow retries if the server doesn't respond or responds with a 5XX status code.

> **State management**
>
> The rendered output in React must be a function of the current state. Therefore, when fetching data from the backend, we need to manage the various states of the fetch. These states start with the fetch loading and progress to success or error states, depending on the result. Assuming the fetch succeeds, there is then the question of how long the data is valid before it needs to be fetched again. All of these states are helpfully managed for us by React-Query.

To do so, we'll first write a wrapper around React-Query's `useQuery`, which is used to fetch data from the backend API, by adding the following to *frontend/src/query.ts*:

```
import axios, { AxiosError } from "axios";
import { useContext } from "react";
import {
  QueryFunction,
  QueryFunctionContext,
  QueryKey,
  useQuery as useReactQuery,
  UseQueryOptions,
  UseQueryResult,
} from "@tanstack/react-query";

import { AuthContext } from "src/AuthContext";

const MAX_FAILURES = 2;

export function useQuery<
  TQueryFnData = unknown,
  TData = TQueryFnData,
  TQueryKey extends QueryKey = QueryKey,
>(
  queryKey: TQueryKey,
  queryFn: QueryFunction<TQueryFnData, TQueryKey>,
  options?: UseQueryOptions<TQueryFnData, AxiosError, TData,
TQueryKey>,
): UseQueryResult<TData, AxiosError> {
  const { setAuthenticated } = useContext(AuthContext);

  return useReactQuery<TQueryFnData, AxiosError, TData,
TQueryKey>(
    queryKey,
    async (context: QueryFunctionContext<TQueryKey>) => {
      try {
        return await queryFn(context);
      } catch (error) {
```

```
        if (axios.isAxiosError(error) && error.response?.status
=== 401) {
            setAuthenticated(false);
        }
        throw error;
    }
    },
    {
      retry: (failureCount: number, error: AxiosError) =>
      failureCount < MAX_FAILURES &&
      (!error.response || error.response.status >= 500),
      ...options,
    },
  );
}
```

This code wraps the standard useQuery hook by checking any errors for a 401-response status code, as shown by the first highlighted block. As a 401-response indicates the user is unauthenticated, the local authentication state is then updated.

The code also provides logic to decide when the request should be retried, as shown by the second highlighted block. The logic will retry the request up to a maximum of two times if there is a network error (no response) or a server error (as indicated by a 5XX response code). Note, therefore, that the query will be in the loading state until all three attempts have failed in the case of network failure.

We'll now add the same logic to React-Query's useMutation, which is used to send data to the backend API by adding the following to *frontend/src/query.ts*:

```
import {
  MutationFunction,
  useMutation as useReactMutation,
  UseMutationOptions,
  UseMutationResult,
} from "@tanstack/react-query";

export function useMutation<
  TData = unknown,
  TVariables = void,
  TContext = unknown,
```

```
>(
  mutationFn: MutationFunction<TData, TVariables>,
  options?: UseMutationOptions<TData, AxiosError, TVariables,
TContext>,
): UseMutationResult<TData, AxiosError, TVariables, TContext> {
  const { setAuthenticated } = useContext(AuthContext);

  return useReactMutation<TData, AxiosError, TVariables,
TContext>(
    async (variables: TVariables) => {
      try {
        return await mutationFn(variables);
      } catch (error) {
        if (axios.isAxiosError(error) && error.response?.status
=== 401) {
          setAuthenticated(false);
        }
        throw error;
      }
    },
    {
      retry: (failureCount: number, error: AxiosError) =>
        failureCount < MAX_FAILURES &&
        (!error.response || error.response.status >= 500),
      ...options,
    },
  );
}
```

This useMutation hook has the same authentication wrapper and retry logic as the useQuery hook.

These two new hooks can then be used in any part of the app in the same way as the standard React-Query hooks are. For example, the useQuery hook can be used like this:

```
import { useQuery } from "src/queries";

const Component = () => {
  const { data } = useQuery(
```

```
      ["key"],
      async () => {
        const response = await axios.get<any>("/");
        return response.data;
      },
    );
    return (<>{ data }</>);
  };
```

We can now fully interact with the backend and store the appropriate state locally, which allows us to focus on giving feedback to the user.

Supporting toast feedback

Toasts (called **Snackbar** in MUI) can be used to show feedback to the user that doesn't relate to a direct element on the page. Good usage of a toast is showing an error message if a request to the backend fails, as shown in *Figure 4.5*, or showing a success message after the user changes their password, as there is no direct confirmation via the page content. A bad usage would be to report that the entered email is invalid as, in this case, the email field should show an error.

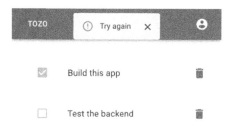

Figure 4.5: An example of a toast error

To support toasts, we need to be able to add a toast from any component in the app and have that toast displayed. Crucially, if there are multiple toasts, they should be displayed one after another so that there is never more than one toast displayed. This is another React context use case, much like the authentication context added earlier. So, let's start by adding the following toast context to *frontend/src/ToastContext.tsx*:

```
import { AlertColor } from "@mui/material/Alert";
import React, { createContext, useState } from "react";

export interface IToast {
```

```
  category?: AlertColor;
  key: number;
  message: string;
}

interface IToastContext {
  addToast: (message: string, category: AlertColor | undefined)
=> void;
  setToasts: React.Dispatch<React.SetStateAction<IToast[]>>;
  toasts: IToast[];
}

export const ToastContext = createContext<IToastContext>({
  addToast: () => {},
  setToasts: () => {},
  toasts: [],
});

interface IProps {
  children?: React.ReactNode;
}

export const ToastContextProvider = ({ children }: IProps) => {
  const [toasts, setToasts] = useState<IToast[]>([]);

  const addToast = (
    message: string,
    category: AlertColor | undefined = undefined,
  ) => {
    setToasts((prev) => [
      ...prev,
      {
        category,
        key: new Date().getTime(),
        message,
      },
```

```
    ]);
  };

  return (
    <ToastContext.Provider value={{ addToast, setToasts, toasts
}}>
      {children}
    </ToastContext.Provider>
  );
};
```

As the `ToastContextProvider` needs to be an ancestor of any of the components that use toasts in the app, we can add it to *frontend/src/App.tsx*:

```
import { ToastContextProvider } from "src/ToastContext";

const App = () => {
  return (
    <QueryClientProvider client={queryClient}>
      <AuthContextProvider>
        <HelmetProvider>
          <Helmet>
            <title>Tozo</title>
          </Helmet>
          <ThemeProvider>
            <ToastContextProvider>
              <Container maxWidth="md">
                <Router />
              </Container>
            </ToastContextProvider>
          </ThemeProvider>
        </HelmetProvider>
      </AuthContextProvider>
    </QueryClientProvider>
  );
}
```

The highlighted lines should be added to the existing code.

Finally, we need to display the toasts. We can do this via a Toasts component, by adding the following to *frontend/src/components/Toasts.tsx*:

```tsx
import Alert from "@mui/material/Alert";
import Snackbar from "@mui/material/Snackbar";
import React, { useContext, useEffect, useState } from "react";

import { ToastContext, IToast } from "src/ToastContext";

const Toasts = () => {
  const { toasts, setToasts } = useContext(ToastContext);
  const [open, setOpen] = useState(false);
  const [currentToast, setCurrentToast] = useState<IToast |
undefined>();

  useEffect(() => {
    if (!open && toasts.length) {
      setCurrentToast(toasts[0]);
      setToasts((prev) => prev.slice(1));
      setOpen(true);
    }
  }, [open, setCurrentToast, setOpen, setToasts, toasts]);

  const onClose = (
    event?: React.SyntheticEvent | Event, reason?: string
  ) => {
    if (reason !== "clickaway") {
      setOpen(false);
    }
  };

  return (
    <Snackbar
      anchorOrigin={{
        horizontal: "center",
        vertical: "top",
```

```
        }}
        autoHideDuration={6000}
        key={currentToast?.key}
        onClose={onClose}
        open={open}
        TransitionProps={{
          onExited: () => setCurrentToast(undefined),
        }}
      >
        <Alert
          onClose={onClose}
          severity={currentToast?.category}
        >
          {currentToast?.message}
        </Alert>
      </Snackbar>
    );
};


export default Toasts;
```

The key aspect of this code is useEffect, which will take a toast from the list of toasts and set it as the current toast whenever there are toasts to display and there isn't an open one. The toasts are also set to automatically close after 6 seconds, giving the user enough time to register it.

We now need to render the Toasts component in the App component, leaving the final version of *frontend/src/App.tsx* as the following:

```
import "@fontsource/roboto/300.css";
import "@fontsource/roboto/400.css";
import "@fontsource/roboto/500.css";
import "@fontsource/roboto/700.css";
import Container from "@mui/material/Container";
import { HelmetProvider } from "react-helmet-async";
import { QueryClient, QueryClientProvider } from "@tanstack/
react-query";


import { AuthContextProvider } from "src/AuthContext";
```

```
import Toasts from "src/components/Toasts";
import Router from "src/Router";
import ThemeProvider from "src/ThemeProvider";
import { ToastContextProvider } from "src/ToastContext";

const queryClient = new QueryClient();

const App = () => (
  <QueryClientProvider client={queryClient}>
    <AuthContextProvider>
      <HelmetProvider>
        <ThemeProvider>
          <ToastContextProvider>
            <Container maxWidth="md">
              <Toasts />
              <Router />
            </Container>
          </ToastContextProvider>
        </ThemeProvider>
      </HelmetProvider>
    </AuthContextProvider>
  </QueryClientProvider>
);

export default App;
```

The highlighted lines are to be added to provide toasts.

Now, when a toast is added by any component, it will show for 6 seconds as an alert snackbar at the top center of the screen.

Summary

In this chapter, we've created a styled frontend that includes routing, validated data entry, and toast feedback, and can connect to the backend API we built in the last chapter. This will allow us to add the specific pages and functionality we need for our to-do app.

The functionality added in this chapter can serve as the basis for any app, not just the one specific to the to-do app being developed in this book. You can take this basis and add any user interface you need for your functionality.

In the next chapter, we'll build the pages and add the functionality that makes up the to-do app.

Further reading

If you find you can't represent the state of your app using React-Query, it is probably time to use a full state management tool such as Redux, `https://redux.js.org`.

Building the Single-Page App

In the previous chapter, we extended a basic React app with the tooling and setup that we require to build user interfaces. This means that in this chapter, we can focus on the functionality that will make up our single-page app. Specifically, we'll add functionality that allows users to authenticate, manage their passwords, and manage their to-dos.

The user interface and functionality to manage user authentication and passwords is useful to any app and could be used directly in yours. While the to-do user interface is unlikely to match what you require in your own apps, the techniques will be applicable.

So, in this chapter, we will cover the following topics:

- Adding navigation
- Adding user authentication pages
- Adding password management pages
- Adding to-do pages

Technical requirements

The following additional folders are required in this chapter and should be created:

```
tozo
└── frontend
    └── src
        └── pages
```

To follow the development in this chapter using the companion repository, https://github.com/pgjones/tozo, see the commits between the tags r1-ch5-start and r1-ch5-end.

Adding navigation

The app we are building needs to allow logged-in users to navigate to the full to-do list, the page allowing them to change their password, and allow them to log out. For logged-out users, they need to navigate between login, register, and reset password pages.

Focusing on the needs of logged-in users, the Material Design system includes an app bar that exists at the top of the page. This will allow for links to the full to-do list (home page) and an account menu to change their password and log out.

> **A more complex navigation**
>
> Your app probably has more pages than the one we are building in this book. This means the navigation system needs to be able to link to more pages. While the account menu can be extended with more links relating to the user, it is not a good location for other links. Instead, a drawer is the best solution. Drawers slide in from the left and can have as many links as required.

The account menu needs to allow users to log out, which means it needs to query the backend via a mutation and then update the app's local authentication context (state). To do so, the following code should be added to *frontend/src/components/AccountMenu.tsx*:

```
import axios from "axios";
import { useContext } from "react";
import { useQueryClient } from "@tanstack/react-query";

import { AuthContext } from "src/AuthContext";
import { useMutation } from "src/query";

const useLogout = () => {
  const { setAuthenticated } = useContext(AuthContext);
  const queryClient = useQueryClient();
  const { mutate: logout } = useMutation(
    async () => await axios.delete("/sessions/"),
    {
      onSuccess: () => {
        setAuthenticated(false);
        queryClient.clear();
      },
    },
  );
```

```
    return logout;
};
```

This code provides a `logout` function, which, when called, triggers the mutation thereby sending a `DELETE /sessions/` request. If this request succeeds, the user is logged out, the local authentication context is set to `false`, and the data stored by `React-Query` is cleared. If the request fails, nothing will change, prompting the user to try again.

With this functionality in place, we now need to add the styled menu. We can do this by adding the following to the existing code in *frontend/src/components/AccountMenu.tsx*:

```tsx
import Divider from "@mui/material/Divider";
import IconButton from "@mui/material/IconButton";
import Menu from "@mui/material/Menu";
import MenuItem from "@mui/material/MenuItem";
import AccountCircle from "@mui/icons-material/AccountCircle";
import React, { useState } from "react";
import { Link } from "react-router-dom";

const AccountMenu = () => {
  const logout = useLogout();
  const [anchorEl, setAnchorEl] = useState<null |
HTMLElement>(null);

  const onMenuOpen = (event: React.MouseEvent<HTMLElement>) =>
    setAnchorEl(event.currentTarget);
  const onMenuClose = () => setAnchorEl(null);

  return (
    <>
      <IconButton
        color="inherit"
        onClick={onMenuOpen}
      >
        <AccountCircle />
      </IconButton>
      <Menu
        anchorEl={anchorEl}
```

```
              anchorOrigin={{ horizontal: "right", vertical: "top" }}
              keepMounted
              onClose={onMenuClose}
              open={Boolean(anchorEl)}
              transformOrigin={{
                horizontal: "right", vertical: "top"
              }}
          >
            <MenuItem
              component={Link}
              onClick={onMenuClose}
              to="/change-password/"
            >
              Change password
            </MenuItem>
            <Divider />
            <MenuItem onClick={() => {logout(); onMenuClose();}}>
              Logout
            </MenuItem>
          </Menu>
        </>
    );
};


export default AccountMenu;
```

This is standard MUI code for a menu that opens when the `IconButton` component is clicked.

We can now add the app bar itself, including a link to the home page, and the account menu if the user is logged in (authenticated) by adding the following to *frontend/src/components/TopBar.tsx*:

```
import AppBar from "@mui/material/AppBar";
import Box from "@mui/material/Box";
import Button from "@mui/material/Button";
import Toolbar from "@mui/material/Toolbar";
import React, { useContext } from "react";
import { Link } from "react-router-dom";
```

```javascript
import { AuthContext } from "src/AuthContext";
import AccountMenu from "src/components/AccountMenu";

const sxToolbar = {
  paddingLeft: "env(safe-area-inset-left)",
  paddingRight: "env(safe-area-inset-right)",
  paddingTop: "env(safe-area-inset-top)",
}

const TopBar = () => {
  const { authenticated } = useContext(AuthContext);

  return (
    <>
      <AppBar position="fixed">
        <Toolbar sx={sxToolbar}>
          <Box sx={{ flexGrow: 1 }}>
            <Button color="inherit" component={Link} to="/">
              Tozo
            </Button>
          </Box>
          {authenticated ? <AccountMenu /> : null}
        </Toolbar>
      </AppBar>
      <Toolbar sx={{ ...sxToolbar, marginBottom: 2 }} />
    </>
  );
};

export default TopBar;
```

The additional padding styling (highlighted) that utilizes the safe-area-inset is required for the app bar to look correct on devices with a notch, such as the iPhone X.

The `TopBar` should be rendered in the `Router` within the `BrowserRouter`, by adding the following to *frontend/src/Router.tsx*:

```
import TopBar from "src/components/TopBar";

const Router = () => (
  <BrowserRouter>
    <ScrollToTop />
    <TopBar />
    <Routes>
      {/* Place routes here */}
    </Routes>
  </BrowserRouter>
);
```

The highlighted lines should be added to the existing code.

Once rendered, the app bar should look like *Figure 5.1*:

Figure 5.1: The app bar as displayed in a mobile browser

With the navigation complete, we can start adding the pages; we will begin by allowing users to register and log in.

Adding user authentication pages

On the first visit to our app, users will need to register, confirm their email, and log in. Whereas, on subsequent visits, they'll just need to log in. Each of these actions will need to be a page in our app.

Registration

The first thing a new user needs to do when visiting our app is to register, so we'll start by adding a registration page. To register, the user will need to enter their email and a password. Once the user has supplied these, we'll use the members API to create the user and then redirect the user to the login page or, if the API call fails, display the relevant error.

We'll start by adding this logic as a custom useRegister hook to *frontend/src/pages/Register.tsx*:

```
import axios from "axios";
import { FormikHelpers } from "formik";
import { useContext } from "react";
import { useNavigate } from "react-router";

import { ToastContext } from "src/ToastContext";
import { useMutation } from "src/query";

interface IForm {
  email: string;
  password: string;
}

const useRegister = () => {
  const navigate = useNavigate();
  const { addToast } = useContext(ToastContext);
  const { mutateAsync: register } = useMutation(
    async (data: IForm) => await axios.post("/members/", data),
  );

  return async (
    data: IForm,
    { setFieldError }: FormikHelpers<IForm>,
  ) => {
    try {
      await register(data);
      addToast("Registered", "success");
      navigate("/login/", { state: { email: data.email } });
    } catch (error: any) {
      if (
        error.response?.status === 400 &&
        error.response?.data.code === "WEAK_PASSWORD"
      ) {
        setFieldError("password", "Password is too weak");
      } else {
```

```
        addToast("Try again", "error");
      }
    }
  };
};
```

The function returned by the `useRegister` hook is designed to be used as a `Formik onSubmit` prop. This allows the function to add a specific error to the password field if the response from the backend indicates the password is too weak (as highlighted). Otherwise, if the registration succeeds, the app navigates to the login page.

> **Automatically logging in on registration**
>
> The flow we've implemented directs the user to the login page where they log in after registering, rather than automatically logging them in. While this isn't the best user experience, it is done to mitigate account enumeration, and hence is a safe default. However, you may decide for your app that the user experience is more important. If so, the backend route will need to log the user in, and this page should direct the user to the home page after registering.

We now need to provide input fields for the user to enter their email and a strong password, which we can ensure by showing the password strength. The fields will be validated to inform the user of any mistakes and use the correct autocomplete values. The autocomplete values should encourage the browser to do most of the work for the user (e.g., by filling in their email address).

The registration page is therefore extended by adding the following code to the existing code in *frontend/src/pages/Register.tsx*:

```
import { Form, Formik } from "formik";
import { useLocation } from "react-router-dom";
import * as yup from "yup";

import EmailField from "src/components/EmailField";
import FormActions from "src/components/FormActions";
import LazyPasswordWithStrengthField from "src/components/
LazyPasswordWithStrengthField";
import Title from "src/components/Title";

const validationSchema = yup.object({
  email: yup.string().email("Email invalid").
required("Required"),
  password: yup.string().required("Required"),
```

```
});

const Register = () => {
  const location = useLocation();
  const onSubmit = useRegister();

  return (
    <>
      <Title title="Register" />
      <Formik<IForm>
        initialValues={{
          email: (location.state as any)?.email ?? "",
          password: "",
        }}
        onSubmit={onSubmit}
        validationSchema={validationSchema}
      >
        {({ dirty, isSubmitting, values }) => (
          <Form>
          <EmailField
            fullWidth label="Email" name="email" required
          />
            <LazyPasswordWithStrengthField
              autoComplete="new-password"
              fullWidth
              label="Password"
              name="password"
              required
            />
            <FormActions
              disabled={!dirty}
              isSubmitting={isSubmitting}
              label="Register"
              links={[
                {label: "Login", to: "/login/", state: { email:
                  values.email }},
```

```
                        {label: "Reset password", to: "/forgotten-
                            password/", state: { email: values.email }},
                    ]}
                />
            </Form>
        )}
        </Formik>
    </>
    );
};


export default Register;
```

As users often forget whether they have already registered, we've made it easier to navigate to the login and reset password pages via the `FormActions` links. In addition, as the user navigates between these pages, any value in the email field is persisted. This saves the user from having to type it in again, hence leading to a better user experience. This is done via the `location.state`, with the `useLocation` hook getting any current value, and the `state` part of the `links` prop of the `FormActions` component setting it.

Then we can add the page to the routing by adding the following to *frontend/src/Router.tsx*:

```
import { Route } from "react-router-dom";

import Register from "src/pages/Register";

const Router = () => (
  <BrowserRouter>
    <ScrollToTop />
    <TopBar />
    <Routes>
      <Route path="/register/" element={<Register />} />
    </Routes>
  </BrowserRouter>
);
```

The highlighted lines should be added to the existing code.

The completed **Register** page should look like *Figure 5.2*:

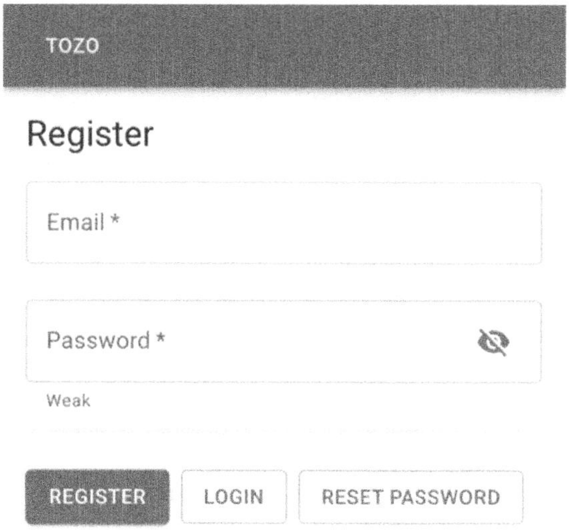

Figure 5.2: The registration page

With users now able to register, they'll next need to confirm their email.

Email confirmation

On registration, users are sent an email with a link back to our app. Within the link is a token that identifies the user. By following the link, the user passes the token to us and proves that they are in control of the email address. Hence, we need a page that, when visited, sends the token to the backend and displays the result.

The link has the form `/confirm-email/:token/` where `:token` is the actual user's token (e.g., `/confirm-email/abcd/`). Therefore, we can extract the token using a route parameter by adding the following to *frontend/src/Router.tsx*:

```
import ConfirmEmail from "src/pages/ConfirmEmail";

const Router = () => (
  <BrowserRouter>
    <ScrollToTop />
    <TopBar />
    <Routes>
      <Route path="/register/" element={<Register />} />
      <Route
        path="/confirm-email/:token/" element={<ConfirmEmail
```

```
/>}
      />
    </Routes>
  </BrowserRouter>
);
```

The highlighted lines should be added to the existing code.

We can now build the ConfirmEmail page and utilize a useParam hook to extract the token from the path. To do so, the following code should be added to *frontend/src/pages/ConfirmEmail.tsx*:

```
import LinearProgress from "@mui/material/LinearProgress";
import axios from "axios";
import { useContext } from "react";
import { useParams } from "react-router";
import { Navigate } from "react-router-dom";

import { useQuery } from "src/query";
import { ToastContext } from "src/ToastContext";

interface IParams {
  token?: string;
}

const ConfirmEmail = () => {
  const { addToast } = useContext(ToastContext);
  const params = useParams() as IParams;
  const token = params.token ?? "";
  const { isLoading } = useQuery(
    ["Email"],
    async () => await axios.put("/members/email/", { token }),
    {
      onError: (error: any) => {
        if (error.response?.status === 400) {
          if (error.response?.data.code === "TOKEN_INVALID") {
            addToast("Invalid token", "error");
          } else if (error.response?.data.code === "TOKEN_
          EXPIRED"){
```

```
                addToast("Token expired", "error");
            }
        } else {
            addToast("Try again", "error");
        }
        },
        onSuccess: () => addToast("Thanks", "success"),
    },
  );


  if (isLoading) {
    return   <LinearProgress />;
  } else {
    return <Navigate to="/" />;
  }
};


export default ConfirmEmail;
```

The highlighted lines show the token parameter being extracted from the path.

To ensure that the user knows that the app is working, a `LinearProgress` bar is shown while the frontend waits for the backend to respond; we can see this in *Figure 5.3*:

Figure 5.3: The Confirm Email page showing a LinearProgress bar to indicate processing is in progress

Finally, after registering and confirming their email, the user will need to log in.

Logging in

Users will need to log in to see and interact with their to-dos. To do so, the user will need to enter their email and a password. Once the user has supplied these, we'll use the session API to create a session. If the login is successful, the user should then be redirected to the home page or to the page given by the `from` state if it is present. The `from` state redirects the user to the page they attempted to view without being logged in.

To do this, we'll start by adding the following logic to *frontend/src/pages/Login.tsx*:

```
import axios from "axios";
import { FormikHelpers } from "formik";
import { useContext } from "react";
import { useLocation, useNavigate } from "react-router";

import { AuthContext } from "src/AuthContext";
import { ToastContext } from "src/ToastContext";
import { useMutation } from "src/query";

interface IForm {
  email: string;
  password: string;
}

const useLogin = () => {
  const location = useLocation();
  const navigate = useNavigate();
  const { addToast } = useContext(ToastContext);
  const { setAuthenticated } = useContext(AuthContext);
  const { mutateAsync: login } = useMutation(
    async (data: IForm) => await axios.post("/sessions/",
      data),
  );

  return async (
    data: IForm,
    { setFieldError }: FormikHelpers<IForm>,
  ) => {
    try {
      await login(data);
      setAuthenticated(true);
      navigate((location.state as any)?.from ?? "/");
    } catch (error: any) {
      if (error.response?.status === 401) {
        setFieldError("email", "Invalid credentials");
```

```
        setFieldError("password", "Invalid credentials");
      } else {
        addToast("Try again", "error");
      }
    }
  };
};
```

With the login logic defined, we can now add the UI elements. This requires a form containing an email and password input, which should be added to the existing code in *frontend/src/pages/Login.tsx*:

```
import { Form, Formik } from "formik";
import * as yup from "yup";

import EmailField from "src/components/EmailField";
import FormActions from "src/components/FormActions";
import PasswordField from "src/components/PasswordField";
import Title from "src/components/Title";

const validationSchema = yup.object({
  email: yup.string().email("Email invalid").
required("Required"),
  password: yup.string().required("Required"),
});

const Login = () => {
  const onSubmit= useLogin();
  const location = useLocation();

  return (
    <>
      <Title title="Login" />
      <Formik<IForm>
        initialValues={{
          email: (location.state as any)?.email ?? "",
          password: "",
        }}
```

```
        onSubmit={onSubmit}
        validationSchema={validationSchema}
    >
      {({ dirty, isSubmitting, values }) => (
        <Form>
          <EmailField
            fullWidth label="Email" name="email" required
          />
          <PasswordField
            autoComplete="password"
            fullWidth
            label="Password"
            name="password"
            required
          />
          <FormActions
            disabled={!dirty}
            isSubmitting={isSubmitting}
            label="Login"
            links={[
              {label: "Reset password", to: "/forgotten-
                password/", state: { email: values.email }},
              {label: "Register", to: "/register/", state: {
                email: values.email }},
            ]}
          />
        </Form>
      )}
    </Formik>
  </>
  );
};

export default Login;
```

The highlighted code shows that the form submission is disabled until the form is dirty. This helps the user as it ensures that they can't submit the form until they have made changes to it. This is a pattern we'll use on all of the forms.

We can now add the page to the routing by adding the following to *frontend/src/Router.tsx*:

```
import Login from "src/pages/Login";

const Router = () => (
  <BrowserRouter>
    <ScrollToTop />
    <TopBar />
    <Routes>
      <Route path="/register/" element={<Register />} />
      <Route
        path="/confirm-email/:token/"
        element={<ConfirmEmail />}
      />
      <Route path="/login/" element={<Login />} />
    </Routes>
  </BrowserRouter>
);
```

The highlighted lines should be added to the existing code.

The completed **Login** page should look like *Figure 5.4*:

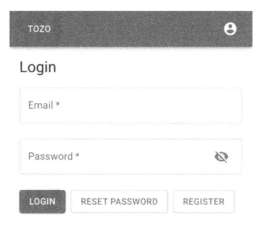

Figure 5.4: The Login page

Users can now register and then log in to our app. They can't manage their password though, which we'll focus on next.

Adding password management pages

We need to allow users to manage their passwords. This is quite involved as users often forget their password and hence a secure mechanism to reset the password is also required.

Changing a password

For the user to change their password, they have to supply their existing password and a strong replacement password. Therefore, the frontend needs to send both to the backend and display relevant errors if the current password is incorrect or the new one is too weak. This logic is contained in the following code, which should be added to *frontend/src/pages/ChangePassword.tsx*:

```tsx
import axios from "axios";
import { FormikHelpers } from "formik";
import { useContext } from "react";
import { useNavigate } from "react-router-dom";

import { ToastContext } from "src/ToastContext";
import { useMutation } from "src/query";

interface IForm {
  currentPassword: string;
  newPassword: string;
}

const useChangePassword = () => {
  const { addToast } = useContext(ToastContext);
  const { mutateAsync: changePassword } = useMutation(
    async (data: IForm) =>
      await axios.put("/members/password/", data),
  );
  const navigate = useNavigate();

  return async (
    data: IForm,
```

```
    { setFieldError }: FormikHelpers<IForm>,
  ) => {
    try {
      await changePassword(data);
      addToast("Changed", "success");
      navigate("/");
    } catch (error: any) {
      if (axios.isAxiosError(error)) {
        if (error.response?.status === 400) {
          setFieldError("newPassword", "Password is too weak");
        } else if (error.response?.status === 401) {
          setFieldError("currentPassword", "Incorrect
            password");
        }
      } else {
        addToast("Try again", "error");
      }
    }
  };
}
```

With the logic defined, we can now add the UI elements. This requires a form containing a plain password field and password strength field as shown here, which should be added to the existing code in *frontend/src/pages/ChangePassword.tsx*:

```
import { Form, Formik } from "formik";
import * as yup from "yup";

import FormActions from "src/components/FormActions";
import LazyPasswordWithStrengthField from "src/components/
LazyPasswordWithStrengthField";
import PasswordField from "src/components/PasswordField";
import Title from "src/components/Title";

const validationSchema = yup.object({
  currentPassword: yup.string().required("Required"),
  newPassword: yup.string().required("Required"),
});
```

```jsx
const ChangePassword = () => {
  const onSubmit = useChangePassword();

  return (
    <>
      <Title title="Change Password" />
      <Formik<IForm>
        initialValues={{ currentPassword: "", newPassword: ""
}}
        onSubmit={onSubmit}
        validationSchema={validationSchema}
      >
        {({ dirty, isSubmitting }) => (
          <Form>
            <PasswordField
              autoComplete="current-password"
              fullWidth
              label="Current password"
              name="currentPassword"
              required
            />
            <LazyPasswordWithStrengthField
              autoComplete="new-password"
              fullWidth
              label="New password"
              name="newPassword"
              required
            />
            <FormActions
              disabled={!dirty}
              isSubmitting={isSubmitting}
              label="Change"
              links={[{ label: "Back", to: "/" }]}
            />
          </Form>
```

```
        )}
      </Formik>
    </>
  );
};


export default ChangePassword;
```

Then we can add the page to the routing by adding the following to *frontend/src/Router.tsx*:

```
import RequireAuth from "src/components/RequireAuth";
import ChangePassword from "src/pages/ChangePassword";

const Router = () => (
  <BrowserRouter>
    . . .
    <Routes>
      . . .
      <Route
        path="/change-password/"
        element={<RequireAuth><ChangePassword /></RequireAuth>}
      />
    </Routes>
  </BrowserRouter>
);
```

In the code block, . . . represents code that has been omitted for brevity.

The completed **Change Password** page should look like *Figure 5.5*:

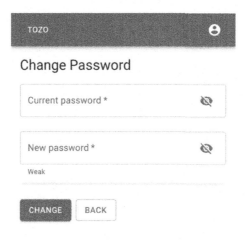

Figure 5.5: The Change Password page

Users can now change their password while logged in. Next, we will allow users to request a password reset link when they have forgotten it.

Forgotten passwords

When a user forgets their password, they'll need to reset it by requesting a reset link. To do so, the user needs to enter their email and then we'll use the members API to send them a password reset email or, if that fails, display a generic error.

The following code to do this should be placed in *frontend/src/pages/ForgottenPassword.tsx*:

```
import axios from "axios";
import { useContext } from "react";
import { useNavigate } from "react-router";

import { useMutation } from "src/query";
import { ToastContext } from "src/ToastContext";

interface IForm {
  email: string;
}
```

```
const useForgottenPassword = () => {
  const navigate = useNavigate();
  const { addToast } = useContext(ToastContext);

  const { mutateAsync: forgottenPassword } = useMutation(
    async (data: IForm) =>
      await axios.post("/members/forgotten-password/", data),
  );

  return async (data: IForm) => {
    try {
      await forgottenPassword(data);
      addToast("Reset link sent to your email", "success");
      navigate("/login/");
    } catch {
      addToast("Try again", "error");
    }
  };
};
```

With the logic defined, we can now add the UI elements. This requires a form containing an email field as shown here, which should be added to the existing code in *frontend/src/pages/ForgottenPassword.tsx*:

```
import { Form, Formik } from "formik";
import { useLocation } from "react-router";
import * as yup from "yup";

import EmailField from "src/components/EmailField";
import FormActions from "src/components/FormActions";
import Title from "src/components/Title";

const validationSchema = yup.object({
  email: yup.string().email("Email invalid").
required("Required"),
});

const ForgottenPassword = () => {
```

```
    const onSubmit = useForgottenPassword();
    const location = useLocation();

    return (
      <>
        <Title title="Forgotten password" />
        <Formik<IForm>
          initialValues={{
            email: (location.state as any)?.email ?? ""
          }}
          onSubmit={onSubmit}
          validationSchema={validationSchema}
        >
          {({ dirty, isSubmitting, values }) => (
            <Form>
              <EmailField
                fullWidth label="Email" name="email" required
              />
              <FormActions
                disabled={!dirty}
                isSubmitting={isSubmitting}
                label="Send email"
                links={[
                  {label: "Login", to: "/login/", state: { email:
                    values.email }},
                  {label: "Register", to: "/register/", state: {
                    email: values.email }},
                ]}
              />
            </Form>
          )}
        </Formik>
      </>
    );
};

export default ForgottenPassword;
```

Then we can add the page to the routing by adding the following to *frontend/src/Router.tsx*:

```
import ForgottenPassword from "src/pages/ForgottenPassword";

const Router = () => (
  <BrowserRouter>
    ...
    <Routes>
      ...
      <Route
        path="/forgotten-password/"
        element={<ForgottenPassword />}
      />
    </Routes>
  </BrowserRouter>
);
```

In the code block, . . . represents code that has been omitted for brevity.

The completed **Forgotten password** page should look like *Figure 5.6*:

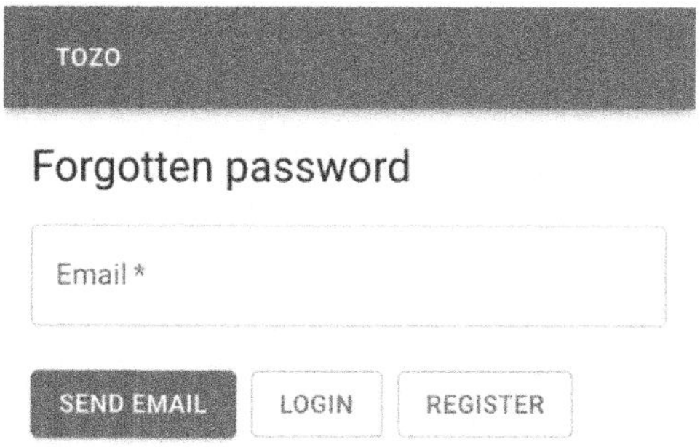

Figure 5.6: The Forgotten password page

Next, we need to add a page for the user to visit to actually reset their password.

Resetting a password

The email sent to the user via the forgotten password page will contain a link to the reset password page. This link will contain a token that identifies the user, in the same way as the email confirmation process described earlier. This page will need to allow the user to enter a new strong password and send it with the link's token to the backend. The logic to do this is shown in the following code, which should be placed in *frontend/src/pages/ResetPassword.tsx*:

```tsx
import axios from "axios";
import { FormikHelpers } from "formik";
import { useContext } from "react";
import { useNavigate, useParams } from "react-router";

import { useMutation } from "src/query";
import { ToastContext } from "src/ToastContext";

interface IForm {
  password: string;
}

interface IParams {
  token?: string;
}

const useResetPassword = () => {
  const navigate = useNavigate();
  const params = useParams() as IParams;
  const token = params.token ?? "";
  const { addToast } = useContext(ToastContext);

  const { mutateAsync: reset } = useMutation(
    async (password: string) =>
      await axios.put(
        "/members/reset-password/", { password, token },
      ),
  );

  return async (
    data: IForm,
    { setFieldError }: FormikHelpers<IForm>,
  ) => {
    try {
```

```
      await reset(data.password);
      addToast("Success", "success");
      navigate("/login/");
    } catch (error: any) {
      if (error.response?.status === 400) {
        if (error.response?.data.code === "WEAK_PASSWORD") {
          setFieldError("newPassword", "Password is too weak");
        } else if (error.response?.data.code === "TOKEN_
          INVALID") {
          addToast("Invalid token", "error");
        } else if (error.response?.data.code === "TOKEN_
          EXPIRED") {
          addToast("Token expired", "error");
        }
      } else {
        addToast("Try again", "error");
      }
    }
  }
};
```

With the logic defined, we can now add the UI elements. This requires a form containing a password field that shows the password's strength. We can do this by adding the following code to the existing code in *frontend/src/pages/ResetPassword.tsx*:

```
import { Form, Formik } from "formik";
import * as yup from "yup";


import LazyPasswordWithStrengthField from "src/components/
LazyPasswordWithStrengthField"
import FormActions from "src/components/FormActions";
import Title from "src/components/Title";

const validationSchema = yup.object({
  email: yup.string().email("Email invalid").
required("Required"),
});
```

```
const ResetPassword = () => {
  const onSubmit = useResetPassword();

  return (
    <>
      <Title title="Reset password" />
      <Formik<IForm>
        initialValues={{ password: "" }}
        onSubmit={onSubmit}
        validationSchema={validationSchema}
      >
        {(({ dirty, isSubmitting, values }) => (
          <Form>
            <LazyPasswordWithStrengthField
              autoComplete="new-password"
              fullWidth
              label="Password"
              name="password"
              required
            />
            <FormActions
              disabled={!dirty}
              isSubmitting={isSubmitting}
              label="Reset password"
              links={[{label: "Login", to: "/login/"}]}
            />
          </Form>
        )}
      </Formik>
    </>
  );
};

export default ResetPassword;
```

Then we can add the page to the routing by adding the following to *frontend/src/Router.tsx*:

```
import ResetPassword from "src/pages/ResetPassword";

const Router = () => (
  <BrowserRouter>
    ...
    <Routes>
      ...
      <Route
        path="/reset-password/:token/"
        element={<ResetPassword />}
      />
    </Routes>
  </BrowserRouter>
);
```

In the code block, . . . represents code that has been omitted for brevity.

The completed **Reset password** page should look like *Figure 5.7*:

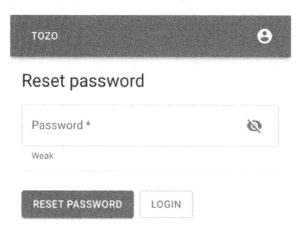

Figure 5.7: The Reset password page

Users can now manage their passwords, which means we can focus on pages to manage their to-dos.

Adding to-do pages

Users will need to manage their to-dos via the app, including creating, editing, and viewing their to-dos. These equate to different pages, which we will add.

First, let's create the specific React-Query queries we will need to fetch to-dos from the backend. We can do this by adding the following code to *frontend/src/queries.ts*:

```
import axios from "axios";
import { useQueryClient } from "@tanstack/react-query";

import { Todo } from "src/models";
import { useQuery } from "src/query";

export const STALE_TIME = 1000 * 60 * 5;   // 5 mins

export const useTodosQuery = () =>
  useQuery<Todo[]>(
    ["todos"],
    async () => {
      const response = await axios.get("/todos/");
      return response.data.todos.map(
        (json: any) => new Todo(json)
      );
    },
    { staleTime: STALE_TIME },
  );

export const useTodoQuery = (id: number) => {
  const queryClient = useQueryClient();
  return useQuery<Todo>(
    ["todos", id.toString()],
    async () => {
      const response = await axios.get(`/todos/${id}/`);
      return new Todo(response.data);
    },
    {
      initialData: () => {
```

```
    return queryClient
      .getQueryData<Todo[]>(["todos"])
      ?.filter((todo: Todo) => todo.id === id)[0];
    },
    staleTime: STALE_TIME,
  },
  );
};
```

The change to the `staleTime` option (highlighted) ensures that `react-query` doesn't continually refetch the to-do data, but rather considers it valid for 5 minutes. This improves the user experience by reducing their internet data usage. In addition, the `useTodoQuery` will helpfully use the cached to-do data as the `initialData` if it is available, thereby saving a request to the backend and improving the user's experience.

> **Which user's to-dos?**
>
> It may not be clear that the `useTodosQuery` defined previously will only return the currently authenticated user's to-dos. This is because we've set up the backend to only return to-dos belonging to the currently authenticated user. It is vital that the authentication decisions are made in the backend as the user is able to alter the frontend code and hence potentially bypass checks.

Next, we need to add the mutations to update the to-do data in the backend by adding the following to *frontend/src/queries.ts*:

```
import { useMutation } from "src/query";

export interface ItodoData {
  complete: boolean;
  due: Date | null;
  task: string;
}

export const useCreateTodoMutation = () => {
  const queryClient = useQueryClient();
  return useMutation(
    async (data: ItodoData) => await axios.post("/todos/",
      data),
    {
```

```
      onSuccess: () => queryClient.
  invalidateQueries(["todos"]),
      },
    );
  };


  export const useEditTodoMutation = (id: number) => {
    const queryClient = useQueryClient();
    return useMutation(
      async (data: ItodoData) =>
        await axios.put(`/todos/${id}/`, data),
      {
        onSuccess: () => queryClient.
          invalidateQueries(["todos"]),
      },
    );
  };


  export const useDeleteTodoMutation = () => {
    const queryClient = useQueryClient();
    return useMutation(
      async (id: number) =>
        await axios.delete(`/todos/${id}/`),
      {
        onSuccess: () => queryClient.
          invalidateQueries(["todos"]),
      },
    );
  };
```

All three of these mutations will invalidate the ["todos"] query data thereby requiring the to-do queries defined previously to fetch the new data, rather than return the outdated data.

With these queries available, we can now create the actual visual elements (i.e., pages for the user to interact with).

Showing to-dos

The first page we need is one to show all the user's to-dos, which is effectively the user's home page. Alongside showing the to-dos, it needs to provide actions to create a to-do and edit and delete any existing ones.

The actions to edit or delete a to-do can be linked to the to-do directly by either clicking on it or a delete button associated with it. However, creating a to-do is a primary action for the page and hence is best suited to a floating action button. Therefore, the to-dos page should look like *Figure 5.8*:

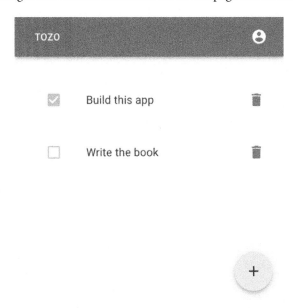

Figure 5.8: The home page showing to-dos, along with the floating action button

First, let's create a component that shows an individual to-do by adding the following to *frontend/ src/components/Todo.tsx*:

```
import Checkbox from "@mui/material/Checkbox";
import IconButton from "@mui/material/IconButton";
import ListItem from "@mui/material/ListItem";
import ListItemButton from "@mui/material/ListItemButton";
import ListItemIcon from "@mui/material/ListItemIcon";
import ListItemText from "@mui/material/ListItemText";
import Skeleton from "@mui/material/Skeleton";
import DeleteIcon from "@mui/icons-material/Delete";
import { format } from "date-fns";
```

```
import { Link } from "react-router-dom";

import { Todo as TodoModel } from "src/models";
import { useDeleteTodoMutation } from "src/queries";

interface IProps { todo?: TodoModel }

const Todo = ({ todo }: IProps) => {
  const { mutateAsync: deleteTodo } = useDeleteTodoMutation();
  let secondary;
  if (todo === undefined) {
    secondary = <Skeleton width="200px" />;
  } else if (todo.due !== null) {
    secondary = format(todo.due, "P");
  }
  return (
    <ListItem
      secondaryAction={
        <IconButton
          disabled={todo === undefined} edge="end"
          onClick={() => deleteTodo(todo?.id!)}
        >
          <DeleteIcon />
        </IconButton>
      }
    >
      <ListItemButton
        component={Link} disabled={todo === undefined}
        to={`/todos/${todo?.id}/`}
      >
        <ListItemIcon>
          <Checkbox
            checked={todo?.complete ?? false}
            disabled disableRipple edge="start" tabIndex={-1}
          />
        </ListItemIcon>
```

```
            <ListItemText
              primary={todo?.task ?? <Skeleton />}
              secondary={secondary}
            />
        </ListItemButton>
      </ListItem>
    );
  }
}
export default Todo;
```

This Todo component will render skeletons if the todo prop is undefined. We can use this to improve the user experience as the to-dos are fetched from the backend.

Skeleton loading

Fetching data from the backend will take a noticeable amount of time, during which the user will wonder what the app is doing. It is therefore best to show the user that the app is working (loading the data). We'll do this by using skeletons, which are gray animated blocks arranged with the same layout as the completed page. The gray arrangement looks like a skeleton, which gives them their name.

The full home page, which shows all the to-dos the user has, is then finished by adding the following to *frontend/src/pages/Todos.tsx*:

```tsx
import Fab from "@mui/material/Fab";
import List from "@mui/material/List";
import AddIcon from "@mui/icons-material/Add";
import { Link, Navigate } from "react-router-dom";

import Todo from "src/components/Todo";
import { useTodosQuery } from "src/queries";

const Todos = () => {
  const { data: todos } = useTodosQuery();

  if (todos?.length === 0) {
    return <Navigate to="/todos/new/" />;
  } else {
    return (
```

```
    <>
      <List>
        {todos !== undefined ?
          todos.map((todo) => <Todo key={todo.id} todo={todo}
/>)
          : [1, 2, 3].map((id) => <Todo key={-id} />)
        }
      </List>
      <Fab
        component={Link}
        sx={{
          bottom: (theme) => theme.spacing(2),
          position: "fixed",
          right: (theme) => theme.spacing(2),
        }}
        to="/todos/new/"
      >
        <AddIcon />
      </Fab>
    </>
  );
  }
};

export default Todos;
```

Then we can add the page to the routing by adding the following to *frontend/src/Router.tsx*:

```
import Todos from "src/pages/Todos";

const Router = () => (
  <BrowserRouter>
    ...
    <Routes>
      ...
      <Route
        path="/"
```

```
            element={<RequireAuth><Todos /></RequireAuth>}
          />
       </Routes>
    </BrowserRouter>
  );
```

In the code block, . . . represents code that has been omitted for brevity.

Now that we can display the to-dos, we need to be able to create and edit them.

Creating to-dos

We will need to provide pages for users to create new to-dos and edit any existing ones. Both these pages will require a form to enter and edit the to-do data. Rather than repeat this form code for each page, we'll create a `TodoForm` component, starting by defining the form validation by adding the following to *frontend/src/components/TodoForm.tsx*:

```
import * as yup from "yup";

const validationSchema = yup.object({
  complete: yup.boolean(),
  due: yup.date().nullable(),
  task: yup.string().required("Required"),
});
```

With the validation schema and form structure defined, we can add the component itself. This component needs only to render the relevant fields within a Formik form. The following code should be added to *frontend/src/components/TodoForm.tsx*:

```
import { Form, Formik } from "formik";

import CheckboxField from "src/components/CheckboxField";
import DateField from "src/components/DateField";
import FormActions from "src/components/FormActions";
import TextField from "src/components/TextField";
import type { ITodoData } from "src/queries";

interface IProps {
  initialValues: ITodoData;
  label: string;
```

```
    onSubmit: (data: ITodoData) => Promise<any>;
}

const TodoForm = ({ initialValues, label, onSubmit }: IProps)
=> (
  <Formik< ITodoData>
    initialValues={initialValues}
    onSubmit={onSubmit}
    validationSchema={validationSchema}
  >
    {(({ dirty, isSubmitting }) => (
      <Form>
        <TextField
          fullWidth label="Task" name="task" required
        />
        <DateField fullWidth label="Due" name="due" />
        <CheckboxField
          fullWidth label="Complete" name="complete"
        />
        <FormActions
          disabled={!dirty}
          isSubmitting={isSubmitting}
          label={label}
          links={[{ label: "Back", to: "/" }]}
        />
      </Form>
    )}
  </Formik>
);

export default TodoForm;
```

We can then use the `TodoForm` in a page to create a to-do task, by adding the following to *frontend/ src/pages/CreateTodo.tsx*:

```
import { useContext } from "react";
import { useNavigate } from "react-router-dom";
```

```
import TodoForm from "src/components/TodoForm";
import Title from "src/components/Title";
import type { ITodoData } from "src/queries";
import { useCreateTodoMutation } from "src/queries";
import { ToastContext } from "src/ToastContext";

const CreateTodo = () => {
  const navigate = useNavigate();
  const { addToast } = useContext(ToastContext);
  const { mutateAsync: createTodo } = useCreateTodoMutation();

  const onSubmit = async (data: ITodoData) => {
    try {
      await createTodo(data);
      navigate("/");
    } catch {
      addToast("Try Again", "error");
    }
  };

  return (
    <>
      <Title title="Create a Todo" />
      <TodoForm
        initialValues={{
          complete: false, due: null, task: ""
        }}
        label="Create"
        onSubmit={onSubmit}
      />
    </>
  );
};

export default CreateTodo;
```

Then we can add the page to the routing by adding the following to *frontend/src/Router.tsx*:

```
import CreateTodo from "src/pages/CreateTodo";

const Router = () => (
  <BrowserRouter>
    . . .
    <Routes>
      . . .
      <Route
        path="/todos/new/"
        element={<RequireAuth><CreateTodo /></RequireAuth>}
      />
    </Routes>
  </BrowserRouter>
);
```

In the code block, . . . represents code that has been omitted for brevity.

The completed Create a Todo page should look like *Figure 5.9*:

Figure 5.9: The Create a Todo page showing the to-do form

Users will want to be able to edit their to-dos after creating them, which we'll add next.

Editing to-dos

Finally, for the to-do pages, we need to allow users to edit their to-dos; you can do this via the following code, which should be added to *frontend/src/pages/EditTodo.tsx*:

```
import Skeleton from "@mui/material/Skeleton";
import { useContext } from "react";
import { useNavigate, useParams } from "react-router";

import TodoForm from "src/components/TodoForm";
import Title from "src/components/Title";
import type { ITodoData } from "src/queries";
import { useEditTodoMutation, useTodoQuery } from "src/
queries";
import { ToastContext } from "src/ToastContext";

interface Iparams {
  id: string;
}

const EditTodo = () => {
  const navigate = useNavigate();
  const params = useParams<keyof Iparams>() as Iparams;
  const todoId = parseInt(params.id, 10);
  const { addToast } = useContext(ToastContext);
  const { data: todo } = useTodoQuery(todoId);
  const { mutateAsync: editTodo } =
useEditTodoMutation(todoId);

  const onSubmit = async (data: ITodoData) => {
    try {
      await editTodo(data);
      navigate("/");
    } catch {
      addToast("Try again", "error");
    }
```

```
  };

  return (
    <>
      <Title title="Edit todo" />
      {todo === undefined ? (
        <Skeleton height="80px" />
      ) : (
        <TodoForm
          initialValues={{
            complete: todo.complete,
            due: todo.due,
            task: todo.task,
          }}
          label="Edit"
          onSubmit={onSubmit}
        />
      )}
    </>
  );
};

export default EditTodo;
```

Then we can add the page to the routing by adding the following to *frontend/src/Router.tsx*:

```
import EditTodo from "src/pages/EditTodo";

const Router = () => (
  <BrowserRouter>
    ...
    <Routes>
      ...
      <Route
        path="/todos/:id/"
        element={<RequireAuth><EditTodo /></RequireAuth>}
      />
```

```
    </Routes>
  </BrowserRouter>
);
```

In the code block, . . . represents code that has been omitted for brevity.

The completed Edit todo page should look like *Figure 5.10*:

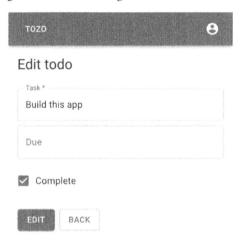

Figure 5.10: The Edit todo page

This completes the frontend functionality we need for our to-do app.

Summary

In this chapter, we've created a user interface that allows users to authenticate, manage their passwords, and manage their to-dos. This completes the development version of the app, which we can now use locally to manage to-dos.

The user authentication and password management user interfaces are useful to any app and could be used directly in your apps, and the to-do user interface could be adapted or used as a reference for other functionality.

In the next chapter, we'll deploy this app to production, allowing users to access and use it.

Further reading

To further enhance your app, I recommend you read more about good UX practices, for example, via https://builtformars.com. Also, to improve your frontend styling skills, I'd recommend https://css-tricks.com.

Part 3
Releasing a Production-Ready App

Building a working app is only the first step; it needs to be deployed to a public domain name that runs on AWS, made secure, and then packaged for the ███████████ ████ all of this by incorporating as many industry best practices as possib███

This part consists of the following chapters:

6

Deploying and Monitoring Your Application

In the previous chapter, we built the frontend of our app, thereby completing it as a useable tool. However, while we are able to use it locally, no other users would be able to. Therefore, in this chapter, we'll deploy our application and make it available via a public domain name, `tozo.dev`. We'll also ensure that we are monitoring the app so that we can quickly fix any issues.

So, in this chapter, you'll learn how to build the infrastructure in AWS for any Docker containerized app that needs a database; this infrastructure will be able to scale to very high loads without major changes. You'll also learn how to set up a **domain name system** (**DNS**) and HTTPS for your domain, both of which are applicable to any website or application. Finally, you'll learn the importance of monitoring and how to do so easily.

For our app to be accessible via a public domain name, it will need to be running on a system that is always accessible via the internet. This could be any system, including our local computer. However, the system needs to be continuously running and accessible via a stable IP address. For this reason, it is much better to pay for a dedicated system managed by AWS.

AWS costs

The AWS infrastructure built in this chapter will cost approximately $20 per month to run without the free tier. It will be cheaper (but not free) if you are able to use the free tier. Alternatively, AWS has a number of startup credit programs you may be eligible for.

If you want to stop paying, you will need to remove the infrastructure, which can be done by deleting the `resource` definitions and running `terraform apply`.

Once we have paid for a remote system, we could configure it to run our app directly, as we have our local system. However, we will use a containerized infrastructure as it is easier to configure the container to run our app than to configure the remote system.

So, in this chapter, we will cover the following topics:

- Making the app production-ready
- Deploying to AWS
- Serving on a domain
- Sending production emails
- Monitoring production

Technical requirements

To follow the development in this chapter using the companion repository, `https://github.com/pgjones/tozo`, see the commits between the `r1-ch6-start` and `r1-ch6-end` tags.

Making the app production-ready

As our production infrastructure will run containers, we need to containerize our app. To do so, we'll need to decide how to serve the frontend and backend, and how to build the container image.

Serving the frontend

So far in development, we've used `npm run start` to run a server that serves the frontend code. This is called **server-side rendering (SSR)**, and we could continue to do this in production. However, it is much easier to utilize **client-side rendering (CSR)**, as this does not require a dedicated frontend server. CSR works by building a bundle of frontend files that can be served by any server (rather than a dedicated frontend server), and we'll use the backend server.

To build the frontend bundle, we can use the `npm run build` command. This command creates a single HTML file (*frontend/build/index.html*) and multiple static files (`css`, `js`, and `media`) in the following structure:

```
tozo
└── frontend
    └── build
        └── static
            ├── css
            ├── js
            └── media
```

The static files, consisting of the files within the *frontend/build/static* folder, can be served by moving the files and structure to the *backend/src/backend/static* folder. Our backend will then serve these files automatically with paths matching the folder structure.

The remaining part of the bundle (i.e., the HTML file) will need to be served for any request that matches a page in the app. To do this, we first need a serving blueprint, which is created by adding the following to *backend/src/backend/blueprints/serving.py*:

```
from quart import Blueprint


blueprint = Blueprint("serving", __name__)
```

The blueprint then needs to be registered with the app, by adding the following to *backend/src/backend/run.py*:

```
from backend.blueprints.serving import blueprint as serving_
blueprint


app.register_blueprint(serving_blueprint)
```

As the backend has no knowledge regarding which paths match the pages on the frontend, it will have to serve the frontend for any paths that do not match backend API paths. This is done in Quart by using a <path:path> URL variable; so, add the following into *backend/src/backend/blueprints/serving.py*:

```
from quart import render_template, ResponseReturnValue
from quart_rate_limiter import rate_exempt


@blueprint.get("/")
@blueprint.get("/<path:path>")
@rate_exempt
async def index(path: str | None = None) ->
ResponseReturnValue:
    return await render_template("index.html")
```

Finally, *frontend/build/index.html* will need to be copied to *backend/src/backend/templates/index.html* for the production app, as we will do when containerizing the app.

As it is now possible to serve the frontend from the backend server, we can now focus on using a production-ready backend server.

Serving the backend

So far in development, we've used `pdm run start` to run and serve the backend. This, however, is unsuitable for production as it starts a Hypercorn server configured for development (for example, it configures the server to output debugging information).

> **Hypercorn**
>
> Quart is a framework that requires a server to work. So far in development, we've been using Hypercorn as configured for development. Hypercorn is a Python server that supports HTTP/1, HTTP/2, and HTTP/3 in a performant manner and is recommended by Quart.

We will configure Hypercorn for production usage using the following placed in *hypercorn.toml*:

```
accesslog = "-"
access_log_format = "%(t)s %(h)s %(f)s - %(S)s '%(r)s' %(s)s
%(b)s %(D)s"
bind = "0.0.0.0:8080"
errorlog = "-"
```

The `accesslog` and `errorlog` configuration ensure that Hypercorn logs every request and error while it runs, which will help us understand what the server is doing. The `bind` configures Hypercorn to listen on the `8080` port, which we'll direct network traffic to when we set up the production infrastructure in the next section.

The server can then be started in production via the following command:

```
pdm run hypercorn --config hypercorn.toml backend.run:app
```

Now we know how to serve the backend in a production environment, we need to focus on how we install everything we need to do so.

Containerizing the app

To run the app in production, we need all the app's dependencies and the app's code installed in the container. We will achieve this by building a container image with the dependencies installed and the code included.

To build the image, we'll use a Dockerfile as it is the clearest way to build an image. Specifically, we will use a multistage Dockerfile, with the first stage building the frontend, and the final stage installing and running the backend server.

> **Docker terms**
>
> A **Dockerfile** is used with Docker to build a container image. The Dockerfile is an ordered list of commands, with each command producing a layer of the final image, and with each layer building upon the previous. The final image will need to include everything required to run the code contained within it. A running instance of the image is known as a **container**.

Building the frontend stage

To build the frontend, we will need a system with NodeJS installed. As this is a common requirement, there are NodeJS base images we can use. Therefore, we can start by adding the following to *Dockerfile* to create a NodeJS-based stage called `frontend`:

```
FROM node:18-bullseye-slim as frontend
```

Next, we need to create a working directory and install the frontend dependencies within it:

```
WORKDIR /frontend/
COPY frontend/package.json frontend/package-lock.json /
frontend/
RUN npm install
```

This is best done before the code is copied into the image as the dependencies change less often than the code.

> **Dockerfile caching**
>
> The Dockerfile is a sequence of commands with each command forming a layer in the final image. These layers are built in the order given in the Dockerfile and a change to any layer requires all the subsequent layers to be rebuilt with earlier layers being cached. Hence, it is best to put layers that rarely change before those that change often.

Finally, we can copy the frontend code we've written for our app into the image and build it with the following code:

```
COPY frontend /frontend/
RUN npm run build
```

We now have a complete frontend stage containing the built frontend. We'll make use of this in the production image.

Building the production image

The production image will be built as the second stage of the *Dockerfile*. This stage can also start from an existing base image, as systems with Python installed are also a common requirement. To do so the following should be added to the *Dockerfile*:

```
FROM python:3.10.1-slim-bullseye
```

Next, we need to add an `init` system to ensure that signals are correctly sent to our backend server as it runs in the Docker container. `dumb-init` is a popular solution and one I've used many times before. `dumb-init` is installed and configured with the following additions:

```
RUN apt-get update && apt install dumb-init
ENTRYPOINT ["/usr/bin/dumb-init", "--"]
```

We can then configure Hypercorn to start when the image is run:

```
EXPOSE 8080
RUN mkdir -p /app
WORKDIR /app
COPY hypercorn.toml /app/
CMD ["pdm", "run", "hypercorn", "--config", "hypercorn.toml",
"backend.run:app"]
```

Next, we need to install the backend dependencies, which first requires that we install pdm and configure Python to work with it:

```
RUN python -m venv /ve
ENV PATH=/ve/bin:${PATH}
RUN pip install --no-cache-dir pdm
```

This allows us to install the backend dependencies using pdm:

```
COPY backend/pdm.lock backend/pyproject.toml /app/
RUN pdm install --prod --no-lock --no-editable
```

Now, we can include the built frontend from the frontend stage:

```
COPY --from=frontend /frontend/build/index.html \
    /app/backend/templates/
COPY --from=frontend /frontend/build/static/. /app/backend/
static/
```

Finally, we can copy the backend code into the image:

```
COPY backend/src/ /app/
```

This gives us a complete image ready to use in production.

To make the image more secure, we can alter the user that will run the server. By default, this is the root user that comes with admin privileges and access, whereas changing to nobody removes these privileges. We can do this by adding the following:

```
USER nobody
```

As we've defined how to build a Docker image, we can now focus on building and deploying it.

Deploying to AWS

To deploy our app, we need to build an infrastructure that runs containers and a database. The containers must be reachable from the public internet, and the database from the containers. This infrastructure is easily buildable with **AWS**, which we'll use. However, in this book, we'll use AWS services that have equivalents on other cloud providers if you wish to use a different provider.

To start, we need to create an AWS account (through this link: aws.amazon.com) using an email, password, and your card details. This account will be the root or superuser account; therefore, we will create an additional **identity and access management** (**IAM**) subaccount for Terraform to use. The IAM user is created via the **Add users** button on the IAM **Users** dashboard shown in *Figure 6.1*:

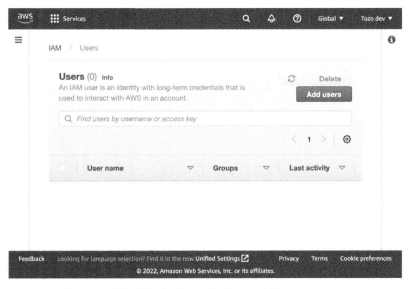

Figure 6.1: The IAM dashboard (with the Add users button)

I will name the user `terraform` to indicate what it is used for. It should have programmatic access only and have the `AdministratorAccess` policy attached. Once created, an access key ID and secret access key will be shown; both need to be added as follows to *infrastructure/secrets.auto.tfvars*:

```
aws_access_key = "abcd"
aws_secret_key = "abcd"
```

I am using `abcd` as examples, which you need to replace with your own values.

With your credentials in place, we can start configuring Terraform to work with AWS. Firstly, add the AWS provider to Terraform by adding the following to the existing Terraform `required_providers` section in *infrastructure/main.tf*:

```
terraform {
  required_providers {
    aws = {
      source  = "hashicorp/aws"
      version = ">=3.35.0"
    }
  }
}
```

After making this change, `terraform init` will need to be run for the change to take effect.

We can then configure the provider, which requires choosing a region to use. As I'm based in London, UK, I'll be using `eu-west-2`, however, I recommend that you use whichever region is closest to your customers. This is done by adding the following to *infrastructure/aws.tf*:

```
variable "aws_access_key" {
  sensitive = true
}

variable "aws_secret_key" {
  sensitive = true
}

provider "aws" {
  access_key = var.aws_access_key
  secret_key = var.aws_secret_key
  region     = "eu-west-2"
}
```

We can now use Terraform to manage the AWS infrastructure, which means we can focus on what we want that infrastructure to be.

Designing the production system

In *Chapter 2, Creating a Reusable Backend with Quart*, we decided to build a three-tier architecture where there is a backend API that communicates with the frontend and with a database. This means that in AWS, we need to be running the database, the backend in a container, and a load balancer to listen to incoming requests from the frontend. To do so, we can use the services and setup shown in *Figure 6.2*:

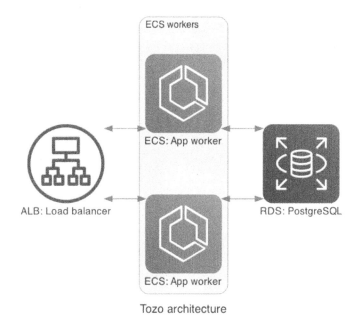

Figure 6.2: The intended AWS architecture

This architecture uses the following AWS services:

- **Relational Database Service (RDS)** to run a PostgreSQ database
- **Elastic Container Service (ECS)** to run the app container
- **Application Load Balancer (ALB)** to accept connections from the internet (frontend)

In addition, we'll use the **Fargate** variant of ECS as this means that we won't need to manage the systems running the containers.

By using these managed services, we can pay AWS to do most of the work of managing the servers, allowing us to focus on our app instead. We can now set up the networking to support this architecture.

Setting up the networking

To build our architecture, we have to start at the foundation, which is the network. We need to define how the systems can communicate with one another. In *Figure 6.3*, you can see that we are aiming for a single **virtual private cloud** (**VPC**) with public and private subnets.

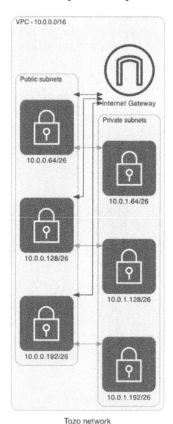

Figure 6.3: The intended network setup

Crucially, the private subnets can only communicate with the public subnets, but not the internet directly. This means that we can place the database in the private subnets, and the app and ALB in the public subnets, thereby adding an additional layer of security that prevents unauthorized database access.

> **VPC**
> A VPC is a virtual network containing resources. We'll use a single VPC for all our resources.

To build the network, we first need to create an AWS VPC for our systems by adding the following to *infrastructure/aws_network.tf*:

```
resource "aws_vpc" "vpc" {
  cidr_block         = "10.0.0.0/16"
  enable_dns_support = true
}
```

CIDR notation

AWS uses **CIDR** block notation to specify the range of valid IPs associated with parts of the network. This notation works by specifying an IP address followed by a number called the netmask (after the /). IPv4 addresses consist of 4 bytes (each byte is 8 bits) with each byte written as a number separated by dots (.). The netmask number indicates how many leading bits of the trial address must match the given address to be considered part of the given range. The following examples show CIDR ranges:

- 10.0.0.0/16 indicates that the first 16 bits (or the first two bytes) must match within this range (i.e., any address starting with 10.0 is in the range)

- 10.0.0.64/26 indicates that the first 26 bits or the first 3 bytes and then the first 2 bits of the final byte must match (i.e., any address between 10.0.0.64 and 10.0.0.128 (excluding 10.0.0.128)

- 0.0.0.0/0 means that any IP address matches

With this VPC setup, all the IP addresses we will use will be in the 10.0.0.0/16 CIDR block and hence will begin with 10.0. This block is a conventional choice for AWS VPCs.

We can now divide the VPC into subnets or subnetworks, as this allows us to restrict which subnets can communicate with each other and the public internet. Firstly, we'll divide the VPC into public subnets in the CIDR block 10.0.0.0/24 and private subnets in 10.0.1.0/24. I've chosen these as blocks as it makes the distinction very clear that any IP that starts with 10.0.0 will be public, and 10.0.1 will be private.

As an AWS region is split into availability zones, we'll create a public and a private subnet for each zone, with up to a total of four subnets. Four is the best number as it is represented by 2 bits and hence makes the CIDR ranges easier to express. The netmask for these subnets is therefore 26, as it is 24 plus the 2 bits required. This is done by adding the following to *infrastructure/aws_network.tf*:

```
data "aws_availability_zones" "available" {}


resource "aws_subnet" "public" {
  availability_zone = data.aws_availability_zones.available.
```

```
names[count.index]
  cidr_block        = "10.0.0.${64 * count.index}/26"
  count             = min(4, length(data.aws_availability_
zones.available.names))
  vpc_id            = aws_vpc.vpc.id
}


resource "aws_subnet" "private" {
  availability_zone = data.aws_availability_zones.available.
names[count.index]
  cidr_block        = "10.0.1.${64 * count.index}/26"
  count             = min(4, length(data.aws_availability_
zones.available.names))
  vpc_id            = aws_vpc.vpc.id
}
```

> **Availability zones**
>
> AWS Regions are split into multiple (usually three) **availability zones** (often called **AZs**). Each zone is a physical data center separated from the others such that if there was a failure of one zone (e.g., a fire), it would not affect the others. Placing our systems in multiple zones, therefore, gives more robustness against failures.

As the *public* name suggests, we want systems in the public subnets to be able to communicate with the internet. This means that we need to add an internet gateway to the VPC and allow network traffic to route between it and the public subnets. This is done by adding the following to *infrastructure/aws_network.tf*:

```
resource "aws_internet_gateway" "internet_gateway" {
  vpc_id = aws_vpc.vpc.id
}


resource "aws_route_table" "public" {
  vpc_id = aws_vpc.vpc.id

  route {
    cidr_block = "0.0.0.0/0"
    gateway_id = aws_internet_gateway.internet_gateway.id
  }
```

```
}

resource "aws_route_table_association" "public_gateway" {
  count           = length(aws_subnet.public)
  subnet_id       = aws_subnet.public[count.index].id
  route_table_id = aws_route_table.public.id
}
```

Finally, in terms of networking, we need a load balancer to accept connections from the internet and route them to the app containers. To begin, let's add a security group for the load balancer that allows inbound (ingress) connections on ports 80 and 443 and any outbound (egress) connection; we do this in *infrastructure/aws_network.tf*:

```
resource "aws_security_group" "lb" {
  vpc_id = aws_vpc.vpc.id

  ingress {
    protocol    = "tcp"
    from_port   = 80
    to_port     = 80
    cidr_blocks = ["0.0.0.0/0"]
  }

  ingress {
    protocol    = "tcp"
    from_port   = 443
    to_port     = 443
    cidr_blocks = ["0.0.0.0/0"]
  }

  egress {
    protocol    = "-1"
    from_port   = 0
    to_port     = 0
    cidr_blocks = ["0.0.0.0/0"]
  }
}
```

> **Protocols and ports**
>
> By default, websites serve requests using TCP (the protocol) on port 80 for HTTP and port 443 for HTTPS. The ports can be changed, but this isn't recommended as most users won't understand how to do the matching change in their browser.
>
> The next version of HTTP, HTTP/3, will use QUIC over UDP as the protocol, with potentially any port the server defines. This technology is in its infancy at the moment though, and hence won't be used in this book.

The load balancer itself can now be added by adding the following to *infrastructure/aws_network.tf*:

```
resource "aws_lb" "tozo" {
  name                = "alb"
  subnets             = aws_subnet.public.*.id
  load_balancer_type  = "application"
  security_groups     = [aws_security_group.lb.id]
}

resource "aws_lb_target_group" "tozo" {
  port        = 8080
  protocol    = "HTTP"
  vpc_id      = aws_vpc.vpc.id
  target_type = "ip"

  health_check {
    path = "/control/ping/"
  }

  lifecycle {
    create_before_destroy = true
  }

  stickiness {
    enabled = true
    type    = "lb_cookie"
  }
}
```

> **Load balancing**
>
> A load balancer will distribute requests across the target group in an attempt to balance the load experienced by each target in the target group. Therefore, it is possible to use multiple machines to serve the requests behind a single load balancer.

With the load balancer in place and ready, we can now start adding systems to the network, starting with the database.

Adding a database

We can now add a PostgreSQL database to the private subnets, and then via a security group, we can ensure that the database can only communicate with systems in the public subnets. This makes it harder for an attacker to gain access to the database as they are unable to access it directly. So, to do this, the following should be added to *infrastructure/aws_network.tf*:

```
resource "aws_db_subnet_group" "default" {
  subnet_ids = aws_subnet.private.*.id
}


resource "aws_security_group" "database" {
  vpc_id = aws_vpc.vpc.id

  ingress {
    from_port   = 5432
    to_port     = 5432
    protocol    = "TCP"
    cidr_blocks = aws_subnet.public.*.cidr_block
  }

  egress {
    from_port   = 0
    to_port     = 0
    protocol    = "-1"
    cidr_blocks = aws_subnet.public.*.cidr_block
  }
}
```

The database itself is created using the `aws_db_instance` Terraform resource, which requires quite a lot of configuration variables to be defined. What is given in the following code is a safe set of variables to run a database that counts in the AWS free tier. The following should be added to *infrastructure/aws.tf*:

```
variable "db_password" {
  sensitive = true
}


resource "aws_db_instance" "tozo" {
  apply_immediately        = true
  allocated_storage        = 20
  backup_retention_period  = 5
  db_subnet_group_name     = aws_db_subnet_group.default.name
  deletion_protection      = true
  engine                   = "postgres"
  engine_version           = "14"
  instance_class           = "db.t3.micro"
  db_name                  = "tozo"
  username                 = "tozo"
  password                 = var.db_password
  vpc_security_group_ids   = [aws_security_group.database.id]
}
```

The db_password should be added to *infrastructure/secrets.auto.tfvars* with a value ideally created by a password generator on a very strong setting (this password will never need to be memorized or typed).

As your app usage grows, I recommend that you change the value of instance_class to a larger machine, enable multi_az to ensure robustness in the case of an availability zone failure, and enable storage_encrypted.

> **AWS web interface**
>
> In this book, we are intentionally defining all the infrastructure as code and ignoring the AWS web interface. This is best as it ensures that we can always restore the infrastructure to a known working state (by running terraform apply) and as it means we have an auditable history of changes. However, it is still very useful to use the web interface to inspect the infrastructure and check everything is as expected.

After running terraform apply, you should see a database running in RDS, which means we can create a cluster to run the app in.

Running the cluster

We will use an ECS cluster to run our Docker images in, and furthermore, we will run the ECS cluster with Fargate as this means we won't have to manage the servers or the cluster itself. While Fargate is not part of the AWS free tier and will sadly cost more, it is worth it to avoid having to manage things ourselves.

Before we can set ECS up though, we first need a repository to place the Docker images in and where ECS will pull and run the images from. We can use the **elastic container register** (**ECR**) for this by adding the following to *infrastructure/aws_cluster.tf*:

```
resource "aws_ecr_repository" "tozo" {
  name = "tozo"
}


resource "aws_ecr_lifecycle_policy" "tozo" {
  repository = aws_ecr_repository.tozo.name

  policy = jsonencode({
    rules = [
      {
        rulePriority = 1
        description  = "Keep prod and latest tagged images"
        selection = {
          tagStatus     = "tagged"
          tagPrefixList = ["prod", "latest"]
          countType     = "imageCountMoreThan"
          countNumber   = 9999
        }
        action = {
          type = "expire"
        }
      },
      {
        rulePriority = 2
        description  = "Expire images older than 7 days"
        selection = {
          tagStatus    = "any"
          countType    = "sinceImagePushed"
```

```
        countUnit   = "days"
        countNumber = 7
      }
      action = {
        type = "expire"
      }
    }
  ]
})
}
```

Alongside creating the repository itself, this ensures that old images are deleted, which is crucial to reducing storage costs over time. Images tagged with prod are kept, as these are applied to the image that should be running (latest is added by Docker to the most recently built image).

Docker image tagging

When a Docker image is built, it can be given tags to identify it. By default, it will be tagged as latest until a newer image is built and takes the tag. It is therefore best to tag images in a useful way to know what they represent.

We can now create the ECS cluster, which requires a task definition and then a service to run the task in the cluster. Starting with the task, we need an IAM role to execute, which we'll call ecs_task_execution, and an IAM role for the task to exist, which we'll call ecs_task. These are created by adding the following to *infrastructure/aws_cluster.tf*:

```
resource "aws_iam_role" "ecs_task_execution" {
  assume_role_policy = jsonencode({
    Version = "2012-10-17"
    Statement = [
      {
        Action = "sts:AssumeRole"
        Principal = {
          Service = "ecs-tasks.amazonaws.com"
        }
        Effect = "Allow"
        Sid    = ""
      }
    ]
```

```
  })
}

resource "aws_iam_role_policy_attachment" "ecs-task" {
  role        = aws_iam_role.ecs_task_execution.name
  policy_arn = "arn:aws:iam::aws:policy/service-role/
AmazonECSTaskExecutionRolePolicy"
}

resource "aws_iam_role" "ecs_task" {
  assume_role_policy = jsonencode({
    Version = "2012-10-17"
    Statement = [
      {
        Action = "sts:AssumeRole"
        Principal = {
          Service = "ecs-tasks.amazonaws.com"
        }
        Effect = "Allow"
        Sid    = ""
      }
    ]
  })
}
```

The policy attachment is used to attach an existing execution policy to the IAM role.

With the roles created, we can now define the ECS task itself. This needs to include all of the environment variables required for the code to run correctly in production. Therefore, an `app_secret_key` variable should be created in the same way as for `db_password` and added to the *infrastructure/secrets.auto.tfvars* file first. Then, the following can be added to *infrastructure/aws_cluster.tf*:

```
variable "app_secret_key" {
  sensitive = true
}

resource "aws_ecs_task_definition" "tozo" {
  family                  = "app"
```

```
  network_mode          = "awsvpc"
  requires_compatibilities = ["FARGATE"]
  cpu                   = 256
  memory                = 512
  execution_role_arn    = aws_iam_role.ecs_task_execution.
arn
  task_role_arn         = aws_iam_role.ecs_task.arn
  container_definitions = jsonencode([{
    name     = "tozo"
    image    = "${aws_ecr_repository.tozo.repository_
      url}:latest"
    essential = true
    environment = [
      {
        name  = "TOZO_BASE_URL"
        value = "https://tozo.dev"
      },
      {
        name  = "TOZO_SECRET_KEY"
        value = var.app_secret_key
      },
      {
        name  = "TOZO_QUART_DB_DATABASE_URL"
        value = "postgresql://tozo:${var.db_password}@${aws_db_
          instance.tozo.endpoint}/tozo"
      },
      {
        name  = "TOZO_QUART_AUTH_COOKIE_SECURE"
        value = "true"
      },
      {
        name  = "TOZO_QUART_AUTH_COOKIE_SAMESITE"
        value = "Strict"
      }
    ]
    portMappings = [{
      protocol      = "tcp"
```

```
        containerPort = 8080
        hostPort      = 8080
      }]
   }])
 }
```

Like with the database, as you gain customers and the app scales up, the `cpu` and `memory` values can be increased to meet the demand.

We have now created the task the service will run; however, before we can create the service, we need to allow connections between the load balancer and the running containers (which are exposing port 8080), by adding the following to *infrastructure/aws_network.tf*:

```
resource "aws_security_group" "ecs_task" {
  vpc_id = aws_vpc.vpc.id

  ingress {
    protocol        = "tcp"
    from_port       = 8080
    to_port         = 8080
    security_groups = [aws_security_group.lb.id]
  }

  egress {
    protocol    = "-1"
    from_port   = 0
    to_port     = 0
    cidr_blocks = ["0.0.0.0/0"]
  }
}
```

This finally allows the service and cluster to be defined by using the following code in *infrastructure/aws_cluster.tf*:

```
resource "aws_ecs_cluster" "production" {
  name = "production"
}


resource "aws_ecs_service" "tozo" {
```

```
name            = "tozo"
cluster         = aws_ecs_cluster.production.id
task_definition = aws_ecs_task_definition.tozo.arn
desired_count   = 1
launch_type     = "FARGATE"

network_configuration {
  security_groups  = [aws_security_group.ecs_task.id]
  subnets          = aws_subnet.public.*.id
  assign_public_ip = true
}
load_balancer {
  target_group_arn = aws_lb_target_group.tozo.arn
  container_name   = "tozo"
  container_port   = 8080
}
lifecycle {
  ignore_changes = [task_definition, desired_count]
}
}
```

The desired_count refers to the number of running containers and should be increased as your app handles more requests; a minimum of three should mean that there are containers running in different availability zones and hence is more robust.

Autoscaling

As the traffic to your app grows, you can scale the infrastructure by allocating larger machines and by increasing desired_count. You should be able to scale to very heavy traffic this way (and many congratulations to you when you do). However, if your traffic is periodic (for example, you have more traffic during the day than the night), then using autoscaling can save costs. Autoscaling is where more resources are allocated automatically as the traffic increases.

We now have the cluster ready to go; all we need now is for the Docker images to be built and placed into the repository.

Adding continuous deployment

With everything ready to run, we can now deploy changes by building the container image, uploading it to the ECR registry, and informing ECS to deploy the new image. This is something that is best done whenever a change is made to the main branch of the GitHub repository. We can do this using a GitHub action, much like in the *Adopting a collaborative development process using GitHub* section in *Chapter 1, Setting Up Our System for Development.*

To start, we need to create an IAM user that has permission to push Docker images to the ECR registry and to inform ECS to deploy a new image. This user will also need an access key, as we'll use this to authenticate the push and deploy commands. The following code creates this user and should be placed in *infrastructure/aws.tf*:

```
resource "aws_iam_user" "cd_bot" {
  name = "cd-bot"
  path = "/"
}


resource "aws_iam_user_policy" "cd_bot" {
  name = "cd-bot-policy"
  user = aws_iam_user.cd_bot.name

  policy = jsonencode({
    Version = "2012-10-17"
    Statement = [
      {
        Action   = "ecr:*"
        Effect   = "Allow"
        Resource = aws_ecr_repository.tozo.arn
      },
      {
        Action   = "ecr:GetAuthorizationToken"
        Effect   = "Allow"
        Resource = "*"
      },
      {
        Action   = "ecs:UpdateService"
        Effect   = "Allow"
        Resource = aws_ecs_service.tozo.id
```

```
    }
  ]
})
}

resource "aws_iam_access_key" "cd_bot" {
  user = aws_iam_user.cd_bot.name
}
```

As the continuous deployment will run as a GitHub action, we need to make this access key and the repository URL available as a `github_actions_secret`; this is done by adding the following to *infrastructure/github.tf*:

```
resource "github_actions_secret" "debt_aws_access_key" {
  repository      = github_repository.tozo.name
  secret_name     = "AWS_ACCESS_KEY_ID"
  plaintext_value = aws_iam_access_key.cd_bot.id
}

resource "github_actions_secret" "debt_aws_secret_key" {
  repository      = github_repository.tozo.name
  secret_name     = "AWS_SECRET_ACCESS_KEY"
  plaintext_value = aws_iam_access_key.cd_bot.secret
}

resource "github_actions_secret" "debt_aws_repository_url" {
  repository      = github_repository.tozo.name
  secret_name     = "AWS_REPOSITORY_URL"
  plaintext_value = aws_ecr_repository.tozo.repository_url
}
```

These secrets can now be used in the continuous deployment action. This action consists of two jobs:

- The first job builds the Docker image and pushes it to the ECR registry
- The second instructs ECS to deploy it (by replacing the currently running image)

Starting with the first job, the following should be added to *.github/workflows/cd.yml*:

```yaml
name: CD

on:
  push:
    branches: [ main ]
  workflow_dispatch:

jobs:
  push:
    runs-on: ubuntu-latest
    env:
      AWS_REPOSITORY_URL: ${{ secrets.AWS_REPOSITORY_URL }}

    steps:
      - uses: actions/checkout@v3

      - name: Configure AWS credentials
        uses: aws-actions/configure-aws-credentials@v1
        with:
          aws-access-key-id: ${{ secrets.AWS_ACCESS_KEY_ID }}
          aws-secret-access-key: ${{secrets.AWS_SECRET_ACCESS_
            KEY}}
          aws-region: eu-west-2

      - name: Login to Amazon ECR
        uses: aws-actions/amazon-ecr-login@v1

      - name: Fetch a cached image
        continue-on-error: true
        run: docker pull $AWS_REPOSITORY_URL:latest

      - name: Build the image
        run: |
          docker build \
            --cache-from $AWS_REPOSITORY_URL:latest \
```

```
                      -t $AWS_REPOSITORY_URL:latest \
                      -t $AWS_REPOSITORY_URL:$GITHUB_SHA .


          - name: Push the images
            run: docker push --all-tags $AWS_REPOSITORY_URL
```

To save on build time, the last built image, tagged as `latest`, is pulled and used as a cache. The built image is then identified by being tagged with the commit hash.

We can now add a `deploy` job that should instruct ECS to deploy the image built for this commit. This is done by adding a `prod` tag to the image already tagged with the commit hash and then informing ECS to run it. This is done by adding the following to *.github/workflows/cd.yml*:

```
  deploy:
    needs: push
    runs-on: ubuntu-latest
    env:
      AWS_REPOSITORY_URL: ${{ secrets.AWS_REPOSITORY_URL }}


    steps:
      - name: Configure AWS credentials
        uses: aws-actions/configure-aws-credentials@v1
        with:
          aws-access-key-id: ${{ secrets.AWS_ACCESS_KEY_ID }}
          aws-secret-access-key: ${{secrets.AWS_SECRET_ACCESS_
KEY}}

          aws-region: eu-west-2


      - name: Inform ECS to deploy a new image
        run: |
          MANIFEST=$(aws ecr batch-get-image --region eu-west-2
--repository-name tozo --image-ids imageTag=$GITHUB_SHA --query
'images[].imageManifest' --output text)
          aws ecr put-image --region eu-west-2 --repository-
name tozo --image-tag prod --image-manifest "$MANIFEST" || true
          aws ecs update-service --cluster production --service
tozo --region eu-west-2 --force-new-deployment
```

This job is idempotent and rerunning it will deploy the specific commit it is associated with. This means it can be rerun to **roll back** a deployment as needed.

> **Deployment issues and rollbacks**
>
> Not every deployment will go well, and the failure could be during the deployment or after deployment. If the deployment itself fails, ECS will automatically keep the previous deployment running. If the failure is after deployment, you can roll back to a safe previous version by rerunning an old `deploy` job.

Now, on every change to the main branch, you should see that change automatically goes live in the production environment. In addition, you can rerun an old `deploy` job if there is a bug or issue with the running job. This is a very productive way of developing an app.

While we can visit the app via the ALB URL, our users will expect to use a nice domain name, which is what we'll focus on next.

Serving on a domain

We'll want a memorable domain name for users to find and identify our app, which means we'll need to buy one from a domain name registrar. I like to use Gandi (`gandi.net`) or AWS as they are trustworthy, however, I like to separate the domain name from the hosting provider in case something goes wrong; for that reason, I'll be using Gandi in this book and have used it to register `tozo.dev` for the next few years, as shown in *Figure 6.4*:

Begin with a domain name. Build your website with Gandi.

Join Gandi and 350,000 users and specifiers.
What is the ideal domain name for your project?

tozo.dev

Transfer your domain names ›   WHOIS ›   💬 Chat with us

Figure 6.4: The Gandi home page for registering a domain

The domain name registrar will allow for the relevant DNS records for a domain name to be specified; to do so with Gandi, we need to add the `gandi` provider to `terraform` by adding the following highlighted code to the existing `terraform` section in *infrastructure/main.tf*:

```
terraform {
  required_providers {
    gandi = {
      source = "go-gandi/gandi"
      version = "~> 2.0.0"
    }
  }
}
```

> **DNS**
>
> While the domain name is memorable for humans, the browser will need a corresponding IP address in order to make the request. This is the purpose of DNS, which will resolve a domain name into the correct IP address. This is done automatically by the browser, but if you'd like to try it manually, you can use the `dig` tool (e.g., `dig tozo.dev`).
>
> A single domain will have multiple DNS records. So far, we've discussed the A record, which contains the IPv4 address for the domain. There is also an AAA record for an IPv6 address, an `ALIAS` record that points to another domain's A or AAA record, an MX record for mail server information (which we'll use in the *Sending production emails* section of this chapter), a CNAME record to alias a subdomain to another domain name, and various others.

Once initialized via `terraform init`, we can start to use `terraform apply` to make these changes. First, we need to retrieve a production API key from Gandi, which is found in the **Security** section as shown in *Figure 6.5*:

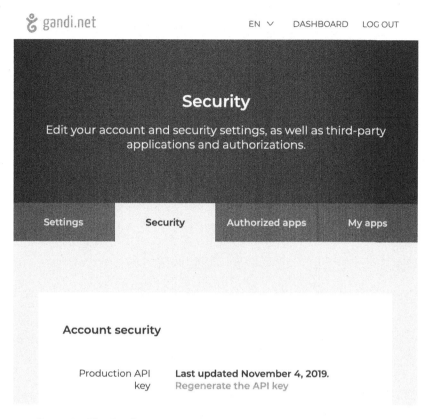

Figure 6.5: The Gandi Security section; note the Production API key section

The API key needs to be added as follows to *infrastructure/secrets.auto.tfvars* (your key will differ from my abcd example):

```
gandi_api_key = "abcd"
```

Then, the key is used to configure the gandi provider by adding the following to *infrastructure/dns.tf*:

```
variable "gandi_api_key" {
  sensitive = true
}

provider "gandi" {
  key = var.gandi_api_key
}
```

The `gandi` provider is now set up and can be used to set DNS records. We need two records: an `ALIAS` record for the domain, and a `CNAME` record for the `www.tozo.dev` subdomain. The following should be added to *infrastructure/dns.tf*:

```
data "gandi_domain" "tozo_dev" {
  name = "tozo.dev"
}

resource "gandi_livedns_record" "tozo_dev_ALIAS" {
  zone   = data.gandi_domain.tozo_dev.id
  name   = "@"
  type   = "ALIAS"
  ttl    = 3600
  values = ["${aws_lb.tozo.dns_name}."]
}

resource "gandi_livedns_record" "tozo_dev_www" {
  zone   = data.gandi_domain.tozo_dev.id
  name   = "www"
  type   = "CNAME"
  ttl    = 3600
  values = ["tozo.dev."]
}
```

With the DNS records in place, we can now focus on adding HTTPS (SSL).

Securing the connection

It is best practice to ensure that communication between the user and the app is encrypted; however, this becomes essential when the communication consists of sensitive information, such as the user's password. As such, we'll only use encrypted communication for our app.

To secure this connection, we can utilize HTTPS using SSL (or TLS), which is widely supported and easy to use. To do so, we need to be issued an encryption certificate that browsers will recognize. Fortunately, Let's Encrypt will issue us a certificate for free. Let's Encrypt is usable with Terraform via the `acme` provider, which is activated by adding the following highlighted code to the existing `terraform` section in *infrastructure/main.tf* and then running `terraform init`:

```
terraform {
  required_providers {
```

```
    acme = {
      source  = "vancluever/acme"
      version = "~> 2.0"
    }
  }
}
```

> **Certificate authorities**
>
> To enable HTTPS, we could create our own self-signed certificate; this would work, but browsers will display a warning. This warning will state that the browser does not trust that the given certificate belongs to the domain. To avoid this warning, we need a recognized certificate authority to sign our certificate. To do so, the certificate authority must confirm that the owner of the domain is the one asking for the certificate. There are many other certificate authorities that charge for this service, but Let's Encrypt does it for free!

To acquire a certificate for a domain name, we'll need to prove to Let's Encrypt that we control the domain name. We can do this via the acme provider by adding the following to *infrastructure/certs.tf*:

```
provider "acme" {
  server_url = "https://acme-v02.api.letsencrypt.org/directory"
}

resource "tls_private_key" "private_key" {
  algorithm = "RSA"
}

resource "acme_registration" "me" {
  account_key_pem = tls_private_key.private_key.private_key_pem
  email_address   = "pgjones@tozo.dev"
}

resource "acme_certificate" "tozo_dev" {
  account_key_pem = acme_registration.me.account_key_pem
  common_name     = "tozo.dev"

  dns_challenge {
```

```
    provider = "gandiv5"

    config = {
      GANDIV5_API_KEY = var.gandi_api_key
    }
  }
}


resource "aws_acm_certificate" "tozo_dev" {
  private_key       = acme_certificate.tozo_dev.private_key_pem
  certificate_body  = acme_certificate.tozo_dev.certificate_pem
  certificate_chain = "${acme_certificate.tozo_dev.certificate_
pem}${acme_certificate.tozo_dev.issuer_pem}"

  lifecycle {
    create_before_destroy = true
  }
}
```

Remember to change the email address, so that reminders and updates from Let's Encrypt go to you rather than to my email!

The certificates we've just created can now be added to the ALB, as doing so will enable users to connect to the ALB, and hence our app, via HTTPS. To ensure only HTTPS is used, let's redirect any visitors that connect via HTTP (port 80) to do so via HTTPS (port 443) by adding the following to *infrastructure/aws_network.tf*:

```
resource "aws_lb_listener" "http" {
  load_balancer_arn = aws_lb.tozo.arn
  port              = "80"
  protocol          = "HTTP"

  default_action {
    type = "redirect"

    redirect {
      port     = "443"
      protocol = "HTTPS"
```

```
      status_code = "HTTP_301"
    }
  }
}
```

We can then accept HTTPS connections and forward them to the target group containing our running app by adding the following code to *infrastruture/aws_network.tf*:

```
resource "aws_lb_listener" "https" {
  load_balancer_arn = aws_lb.tozo.arn
  port              = 443
  protocol          = "HTTPS"
  ssl_policy        = "ELBSecurityPolicy-2016-08"
  certificate_arn   = aws_acm_certificate.tozo_dev.arn

  default_action {
    type             = "forward"
    target_group_arn = aws_lb_target_group.tozo.arn
  }
}
```

With these changes, you can run the following:

```
terraform init
terraform apply
```

This should create all the infrastructure. You will then need to push your local code to the GitHub repository for the CD job to run and deploy the app. Once that completes, you should be able to visit `tozo.dev` (or whatever your domain is) and see the running app. We can now focus on how we can send emails, such as a welcome email, to the app's users.

Sending production emails

In the *Sending emails* section of *Chapter 2, Creating a Reusable Backend with Quart,* we configured our app to send emails via Postmark if a POSTMARK_TOKEN configuration value was present. We can now set up production so that there is a POSTMARK_TOKEN in the app's configuration.

To do so, we first need approval from Postmark; this is done to ensure that we don't intend to misuse their service. As we are using Postmark for transactional emails (e.g., password reset tokens), we should get permission. This is gained via the request approval button or by talking directly to their support.

With permission granted, we can add the relevant DNS records to prove to Postmark that we control the `tozo.dev` domain. These are available from your Postmark account and should be added as follows to *infrastructure/dns.tf*:

```
resource "gandi_livedns_record" "tozo_dev_DKIM" {
  zone    = data.gandi_domain.tozo_dev.id
  name    = "20210807103031pm._domainkey"
  type    = "TXT"
  ttl     = 10800
  values  = ["k=rsa;p=abcd"]
}


resource "gandi_livedns_record" "tozo_dev_CNAME" {
  zone    = data.gandi_domain.tozo_dev.id
  name    = "pm-bounces"
  type    = "CNAME"
  ttl     = 10800
  values  = ["pm.mtasv.net."]
}
```

Note the highlighted `abcd` DKIM value is a placeholder and should be replaced with your own value.

The Postmark token we need is also available in your account and should be added to *infrastructure/secrets.auto.tfvars* (your key will differ from my `abcd` example):

```
postmark_token = "abcd"
```

To make this token available to our app, we need it to be an environment variable in the running container. This is achieved by adding the following to the existing `aws_ecs_task_definition` section in *infrastructure/aws_cluster.tf*:

```
variable "postmark_token" {
  sensitive = true
}


resource "aws_ecs_task_definition" "tozo" {
  container_definitions = jsonencode([{
    environment = [
      {
```

```
        name  = "TOZO_POSTMARK_TOKEN"
        value = var.postmark_token
      }
    ]
  }])
}
```

The highlighted lines should be added to the file. Note that the environment variable name is TOZO_POSTMARK_TOKEN as only environment variables prefixed with TOZO_ are loaded into the app's configuration. See the *Creating a basic Quart app* section in *Chapter 2, Creating a Reusable Backend with Quart*.

Our app should now send the welcome, reset password, and other emails using Postmark. We can monitor this by logging into Postmark and checking the activity. Next, we can focus on monitoring the app itself.

Monitoring production

Now that our app is running in production, we need to keep it working. This means we need to monitor for issues, notably errors and slow performance, as both lead to a poor user experience. To do so, I find it easiest to use Sentry (sentry.io), which can monitor errors and performance in the frontend and backend code.

Monitoring the backend

To monitor the backend, we should create a new project in Sentry and call it backend. This is where we'll see any errors and can monitor the performance. The project will have its own **data source name** (**DSN**) value, which we'll need to provide to the app in production. The DSN is found on the project's configuration page on sentry.io.

To make the DSN available to our app, we need it to be an environment variable in the running container. This is achieved by adding the following to the existing aws_ecs_task_definition section in *infrastructure/aws_cluster.tf*:

```
resource "aws_ecs_task_definition" "tozo" {
  container_definitions = jsonencode([{
    environment = [
      {
        name  = "SENTRY_DSN"
        value = "https://examplePublicKey@o0.ingest.sentry.
io/0"
```

```
        }
    ]
  }])
}
```

The highlighted value will be different for your setup, as the value used here is Sentry's example DSN.

We next need to install `sentry-sdk` by running the following in the *backend* folder:

```
pdm add sentry-sdk
```

This allows us to activate the Sentry monitoring for Quart using Sentry's `QuartIntegration`; we can do this by adding the following to *backend/src/backend/run.py*:

```
import sentry_sdk
from sentry_sdk.integrations.quart import QuartIntegration

if "SENTRY_DSN" in os.environ:
    sentry_sdk.init(
        dsn=os.environ["SENTRY_DSN"],
        integrations=[QuartIntegration()],
        traces_sample_rate=0.2,
    )
app = Quart(__name__)
```

It is important that `sentry_sdk.init` is before `app = Quart(__name__)`, as highlighted in the previous code.

> **Expected performance**
>
> As a rule of thumb, if an action takes more than 100 milliseconds to return a response, the user will notice the slowdown and have a bad experience. Therefore, I aim to have routes completed within 40 milliseconds, as this gives time for the network transmission and any UI updates to take place within the 100 millisecond target. There is an exception though, which is that any route that hashes the password should take in excess of 100 milliseconds – otherwise, the hash is too weak and liable to be broken.

...d to monitor the backend, so now we can do the same for the frontend.

Monitoring the frontend

To monitor the frontend, we first need to create a frontend project in Sentry. Next, we need to install the Sentry SDK by running the following in the *frontend* folder:

```
npm install @sentry/react @sentry/tracing
```

This allows us to activate the Sentry monitoring using Sentry's browser integration by adding the following to *frontend/src/index.tsx*:

```
import * as Sentry from "@sentry/react";
import { BrowserTracing } from "@sentry/tracing";

if (process.env.NODE_ENV === "production") {
  Sentry.init({
    dsn: "https://examplePublicKey@o0.ingest.sentry.io/0",
    integrations: [new BrowserTracing()],
    tracesSampleRate: 0.2,
  });
}
```

The highlighted DSN value provided is an example, and yours is available in the project settings on sentry.io. As this value isn't sensitive, it is safe for us to place it directly in the frontend code.

To work correctly, it is important that Sentry.init is before the following:

```
const root = ReactDOM.createRoot(
  document.getElementById("root") as HTMLElement,
);
```

And that is all we need to monitor the frontend. Next, we can show the user a friendly error page when an error occurs.

Displaying an error page

It is likely, despite our best efforts, that users will encounter bugs and errors as they use the app. When this happens, we should show the user a helpful error page that acknowledges the issue and encourages the user to try again, as shown in *Figure 6.6*:

> (!) Error
>
> Sorry, something has gone wrong. Please try
> reloading the page or click here.

Figure 6.6: The Error page

This page is implemented by adding the following code to *frontend/src/pages/Error.tsx*:

```tsx
import Alert from "@mui/material/Alert";
import AlertTitle from "@mui/material/AlertTitle";
import Container from "@mui/material/Container";
import Link from "@mui/material/Link";

const Error = () => (
  <Container maxWidth="sm">
    <Alert severity="error" sx={{ marginTop: 2 }}>
      <AlertTitle>Error</AlertTitle>
        Sorry, something has gone wrong.
        Please try reloading the page or click{" "}
        <Link href="/">here</Link>.
    </Alert>
  </Container>
);

export default Error;
```

Error tolerance

In my experience, users are very tolerant of bugs that are acknowledged and fixed quickly, with the inconvenience being quickly forgotten. However, bugs that are not acknowledged or affect the user multiple times are not forgiven and result in the user using a different app. This is why it is vital to monitor the app for errors and fix them first, before adding any new features.

To display this error page when an error occurs, we can use Sentry's ErrorBoundary by making the following changes to *frontend/src/index.tsx*:

```
import Error from "src/pages/Error";

root.render(
  <React.StrictMode>
    <Sentry.ErrorBoundary fallback={<Error />}>
      <App />
    </Sentry.ErrorBoundary>
  </React.StrictMode>,
);
```

To check that everything is set up and works correctly, we can create a route that errors when visited by adding the following to *frontend/src/Router.tsx*:

```
const ThrowError = () => {throw new Error("Test Error")};

const Router = () => (
  <BrowserRouter>
    ...
    <Routes>
      ...
      <Route
        element={<ThrowError />}
        path="/test-error/"
      />
    </Routes>
  </BrowserRouter>
);
```

In the code block, . . . represents code that has been omitted for brevity.

Now, any visit to /test-error/ will result in an error and the error page being displayed.

With a friendly error page and Sentry installed, we are able to monitor for errors and performance issues.

Summary

In this chapter, we've deployed our app to the cloud and served it on our own memorable domain name, thereby allowing any user to use our app. We also learned how to monitor it for any issues, and so are ready to fix bugs as quickly as possible.

The infrastructure we've built in this chapter can be used for any containerized app that needs a database and will scale to very high loads.

In the next chapter, we'll add some advanced features to our app and turn it into a progressive web app.

7

Securing and Packaging the App

In the previous chapter, we deployed our app to `tozo.dev`, allowing users to use our web app via a browser on any device, and added monitoring so that we know when things go wrong.

In this chapter, we will focus on how we can keep our app secure, both in terms of the code we use and the methods users use to authenticate. We'll also package our app so that users can use our app via the app stores.

It is important to view the app's security as a continual process, whereby the practices and packages must be continually updated and improved. In this chapter, I'll demonstrate my process for managing package updates, which you can adopt and improve upon. We'll also adopt current best practices to secure the app.

We'll also make a major change to support multifactor authentication. While this will allow users to opt-in for greater security, it will also show how to make large changes to the app; specifically, it will show how to alter the database via a migration.

Finally, by packaging our app, we can allow our users to find our app in the app stores and use it as they would any other app on their phone.

So, in this chapter, we will cover the following topics:

- Securing the app
- Updating packages
- Adding multifactor authentication
- Converting to a progressive web app

Technical requirements

To follow the development in this chapter using the companion repository, `https://github.com/pgjones/tozo`, see the commits between the `r1-ch7-start` and `r1-ch7-end` tags.

Securing the app

Much of what we've done so far uses secure defaults (for example, the Strict SameSite setting used in *Chapter 2, Creating a Reusable Backend with Quart*), however, there is always more than can be done to secure an app. Specifically, we can utilize secure headers to limit what the browser will allow the page to do, further protect against account enumeration, and limit the accounts that can register to limit spam. Let's look at those security options now.

Adding secure headers

To further secure our app, we can utilize additional secure headers to limit what the browser will allow the app to do. These headers should be added to every response the app sends; we can do this by adding the following to *backend/src/backend/run.py*:

```python
from quart import Response
from werkzeug.http import COOP


@app.after_request
async def add_headers(response: Response) -> Response:
    response.content_security_policy.default_src = "'self'"
    response.content_security_policy.connect_src = "'self' *.sentry.io"
    response.content_security_policy.frame_ancestors = "'none'"
    response.content_security_policy.report_uri = "https://ingest.sentry.io"
    response.content_security_policy.style_src = "'self' 'unsafe-inline'"
    response.cross_origin_opener_policy = COOP.SAME_ORIGIN
    response.headers["Referrer-Policy"] = "no-referrer, strict-origin-when-cross-origin"
    response.headers["X-Content-Type-Options"] = "nosniff"
    response.headers["X-Frame-Options"] = "SAMEORIGIN"
    response.headers[
        "Strict-Transport-Security"
```

```
    ] = "max-age=63072000; includeSubDomains; preload"
    return response
```

The highlighted value of `report_uri` given as "`https://ingest.sentry.io`" is a placeholder, and the correct value for your usage can be found in the CSP section of the Sentry dashboard for the backend project.

The secure headers added are as follows:

- `Content-Security-Policy` (CSP): This is used to limit how the content can interact with the page and other domains. As used, it restricts the content such that it must have been served by our domain (called `self`) with the exception of any styling content that can also be added inline (called `unsafe-inline`) as required for MUI to work correctly. The setup also allows connections to `sentry.io` so that our monitoring can work. Finally, it has a reporting URI so that we can monitor any errors with the CSP itself.

- `Cross-Origin-Opener-Policy` (COOP): This isolates our app from other domains (origins).

- `Referrer-Policy`: This restricts how the browser can populate the `Referer` header when following links and is used to protect the user's privacy.

- `X-Content-Type-Options`: This ensures that the browser respects the `content` type we return from the server.

- `X-Frame-Options`: This improves protection against clickjacking and ensures that our app is only displayed on our domain.

- `Strict-Transport-Security`: This informs the browser that all subsequent connections to our app must be done over HTTPS.

> **OWASP**
>
> The authoritative source for web application security best practices is the **OWASP** foundation, which can be found here: `owasp.org`. The header recommendations in this book are based on their recommendations.

With the secure headers in place, we can look in more detail at how we log users in while protecting against account enumeration.

Protecting against account enumeration

Account enumeration is where an attacker attempts to learn what email addresses are used as registered accounts. By doing so, the attacker can learn who uses a sensitive app (e.g., a dating app) and can learn which accounts they can try to force access to. Protecting against this requires compromises in the user experience, as we discussed in the *Adding user authentication pages* section of *Chapter 5, Building the Single-Page App*, in reference to auto logins on registration.

In this book, we'll adopt the most secure practices possible, which means we need to revisit the login functionality implemented in the *Building the session API* section of *Chapter 3, Building the API*, as it is susceptible to account enumeration attacks.

The weakness in the login functionality is due to the code only checking the password hash if the given email belongs to a registered member. This means that the route takes significantly longer to respond to emails belonging to registered members than for emails that don't; this allows an attacker to time the response to understand whether the email is registered or not. Therefore, the mitigation is to always check a password hash, by changing the route in *backend/src/backend/blueprints/sessions.py* to the following:

```python
REFERENCE_HASH = "$2b$12$A.BRD7hCbGciBiqNRTqxZ.odBxGo.
XmRmgN4u9Jq7VUkW9xRmPxK."


@blueprint.post("/sessions/")
@rate_limit(5, timedelta(minutes=1))
@validate_request(LoginData)
async def login(data: LoginData) -> ResponseReturnValue:
    """Login to the app.

    By providing credentials and then saving the
    returned cookie.
    """
    result = await select_member_by_email(
        g.connection, data.email
    )
    password_hash = REFERENCE_HASH
    if result is not None:
        password_hash = result.password_hash

    passwords_match = bcrypt.checkpw(
        data.password.encode("utf-8"),
        password_hash.encode("utf-8"),
```

```
    )
    if passwords_match and result is not None:
        login_user(AuthUser(str(result.id)), data.remember)
        return {}, 200
    else:
        raise APIError(401, "INVALID_CREDENTIALS")
```

REFERENCE_HASH is set to a very long random string of characters that is extremely unlikely to be matched by chance.

With the additional protection against account enumeration, we can focus on the accounts themselves by adding protection against spam accounts.

Protecting against spam accounts

If you allow users to register and interact with your app, it is inevitable that you will have users that will use it to spam you or other users. An easy initial mitigation against this is to prevent users from registering to your app with disposable email addresses (these are free short-lived email addresses that are perfect for spammers). Fortunately, the disposable-email-domains project keeps a track of these domains and is installed by running the following in the *backend* directory:

```
pdm add disposable-email-domains
```

The following can then be added to the start of the register route in *backend/src/backend/blueprints/members.py*:

```
from disposable_email_domains import blocklist  # type: ignore

async def register(data: MemberData) -> ResponseReturnValue:
    email_domain = data.email.split("@", 1)[1]
    if email_domain in blocklist:
        raise APIError(400, "INVALID_DOMAIN")
    ...
```

In the previous code block, . . . represents the existing register code. This will block registrations from the blocked email domains by returning an appropriate error code.

Now, we need to handle this error in the useRegister hook found in *frontend/src/pages/Register.tsx*:

```
const useRegister = () => {
    ...
    if (
```

```
        error.response?.status === 400 &&
        error.response?.data.code === "WEAK_PASSWORD"
    ) {
        setFieldError("password", "Password is too weak");
    } else if (
        error.response?.status === 400 &&
        error.response?.data.code === "INVALID_DOMAIN"
    ) {
        setFieldError("email", "Invalid email domain");
    } else {
        addToast("Try again", "error");
    }
    ...
}
```

The highlighted lines are the existing code in the `useRegister` hook. It is important that the check is added as an `else if` clause to the existing `if` clause (as shown in this snippet), otherwise the user may get multiple confusing error messages.

Keeping an app secure is in practice an arms race against attackers, and I recommend you continue to follow OWASP and adopt the latest guidance. Likewise, we'll need to keep updating our packages, which we'll focus on next.

Updating packages

A very common source of vulnerabilities in web applications is vulnerable dependent packages. This is especially true if the application is using an older version of a package when a new, more secure version is available. To mitigate against this, we can periodically check for known vulnerabilities and, crucially, update the packages as often as possible.

Importance of lockfiles

By using npm and PDM, we are using lockfiles; this means that we'll always install the same package version on any system until we change the lockfile. Without a lockfile, we would quickly be in a position where different systems run with different package versions and potentially different packages. This would make it hard to diagnose bugs, as it may depend on a version we aren't testing. Crucially though, it would make our app less secure as we would have no control over what was installed.

Periodically checking for vulnerabilities

In our app, we are using many third-party dependencies, each of which is likely to be using additional third-party dependencies. This means there is a large number of libraries that we need to check for vulnerabilities – too many to do ourselves! Fortunately, when others find vulnerabilities, they are published, and tools exist to check the version installed against the published list of issues.

We'll use these tools to check our code, allowing us to switch to a fixed version if they find anything. This is something I recommend to be done periodically and automatically, specifically every week, via a GitHub workflow.

To start, we can create a workflow that is scheduled to run at 9 a.m. UTC on a Tuesday by adding the following to *.github/workflows/audit.yml*:

```
name: Audit

on:
  schedule:
    - cron: "0 9 * * 2"

jobs:
```

> **Tuesday patches**
>
> Tuesday is typically the day to apply patches as it's early in the week, almost always a workday (Mondays may not be workdays during holidays), and crucially, gives time on Monday to respond to weekend issues, leaving Tuesday free for patch issues.

To check the frontend code, we can use npm audit, which is built into the npm package manager. This tool will check the installed frontend dependencies and alert if any insecure package versions are found. To run it on the schedule, the following job should be added to *.github/workflows/audit.yml*:

```
frontend-audit:
  runs-on: ubuntu-latest

  defaults:
    run:
      working-directory: frontend

  steps:
    - name: Use Node.js
```

```
      uses: actions/setup-node@v2
      with:
        node-version: '18'

    - uses: actions/checkout@v3

    - name: Initialise dependencies
      run: npm ci --cache .npm --prefer-offline

    - name: Audit the dependencies
      run: npm audit
```

Now, to check the backend code, we can use pip-audit, which is installed by running the following command in the *backend* directory:

pdm add --dev pip-audit

We'll add a pdm script so that we can use pdm run audit to audit the code, as we did in the *Installing Python for backend development* section of *Chapter 1, Setting Up Our System for Development;* so, add the following to *backend/pyproject.toml*:

```
[tool.pdm.scripts]
audit = "pip-audit"
```

With this in place, we can add the following job to *.github/workflows/audit.yml*:

```
  backend-audit:
    runs-on: ubuntu-latest

    defaults:
      run:
        working-directory: backend

    steps:
      - uses: actions/checkout@v3

      - uses: actions/setup-python@v4
        with:
```

```
        python-version: '3.10'

    - name: Initialise dependencies
      run: |
        pip install pdm
        pdm install

    - name: Audit the dependencies
      run: pdm run audit
```

This workflow will fail if either the `frontend-audit` or `backend-audit` job finds packages with security issues, and will alert us. However, it is best to be proactive and keep our dependencies up to date.

A system for monthly updates

To ensure the dependencies are up to date, I recommend updating all the packages every month. This ensures that the app never has dependencies that are more than a month old and makes it easier to utilize the dependencies' latest features. This may seem like a lot of work, however, in my experience, it takes much more effort to do all the upgrades at once than to do them in smaller batches.

To make this process easier, we must unpin the dependencies in the *frontend/package.json* and *backend/pyproject.toml* files. This doesn't mean we've unpinned the dependencies though, as both *frontend/package-lock.json* and *backend/pdm.lock* will fully define the exact versions to install. It instead means that we will allow our app to work with any library version if directed – and we will direct it to always use the latest.

The *frontend/package.json* file should look like this:

```
"dependencies": {
  "@emotion/react": "*",
  "@emotion/styled": "*",
    ...
},
"devDependencies": {
  "@types/zxcvbn": "*",
  "eslint": "*",
    ...
}
```

Note that each dependency is now unpinned, with * meaning any version is allowed.

With these changes made, we can run the following command in the *frontend* directory to update the frontend dependencies:

```
npm update
```

We can also run a similar command in the *backend* directory to update the backend dependencies:

```
pdm update
```

Finally, to upgrade the infrastructure dependencies, the following should be run in the *infrastructure* directory:

```
terraform init -upgrade
```

These updates will likely result in small changes needing to be made to support the latest versions. It is likely that the CI checks, especially the type checking we've used throughout, will warn if these changes are not made.

Now that we have a system for keeping our app up to date, we can add multifactor authentication to help our users secure their accounts.

Adding multifactor authentication

Our app allows users to log in by providing an email and a password. This means we allow them to authenticate with something they know (i.e., the password). We could also allow them to use other factors of authentication such as using their fingerprint (i.e., something they are), or a specific mobile device (i.e., something they have). Requiring a user to authenticate using multiple factors makes it much harder for an attacker to gain access to their account, however, it also makes it harder for the user to authenticate themselves. Therefore, it is best to allow users to opt into multifactor authentication.

Users are most familiar with using their phones as an additional factor, which we will implement using **time-based one-time passcode (TOTP)** tokens based on a shared secret. The shared secret, on the user's phone, is an additional factor. It is also common to use SMS messages sent to the user's phone; however, this method is increasingly easy to attack and should not be considered secure.

> **TOTP**
>
> The TOTP algorithm makes use of a shared secret and the current time to generate a code that is valid for a certain period of time (usually about 60 seconds). Any two systems should calculate the same code for the same time and shared secret, hence the user can provide a code that our app should match.

Multifactor Authentication (MFA) using TOTP works by first sharing a secret with the user. This is typically done by showing a QR code in our app, which the user scans using an authentication app.

The user's authentication app will then display a code that the user can enter in our app to confirm that MFA has been set up. Then, on any subsequent logins, the user will need to enter the current code as displayed by their authentication app.

To support MFA in our app, we will need to update the database and associated models, add the functionality to activate it in the backend and frontend, and then, finally, utilize MFA when logging in.

Updating the database and models

To support MFA, we need to store two pieces of information for each member:

- The first is the shared secret, which can be NULL if the user hasn't activated MFA.

- The second is the last code they used, which can also be NULL. The last code is required to prevent replay attacks whereby an attacker simply resends the previous MFA code.

To add this information, we need to create a new database migration by adding the following code to *backend/src/backend/migrations/1.py*:

```
from quart_db import Connection


async def migrate(connection: Connection) -> None:
    await connection.execute(
        "ALTER TABLE members ADD COLUMN totp_secret TEXT"
    )
    await connection.execute(
        "ALTER TABLE members ADD COLUMN last_totp TEXT"
    )


async def valid_migration(connection: Connection) -> bool:
    return True
```

> **Good migrations**
>
> Database migrations must be written with care, as the migration will change the database state while the code is accessing it. For this reason, it is best to write migrations that add functionality while allowing older code to continue to run. For example, it is best not to delete or rename columns in one migration; instead, a new column should be added, then used for a while before the old column is removed.

We also need to update the backend model to account for these two new columns, by changing the Member model in *backend/src/backend/models/member.py* to the following (changes are highlighted):

```python
@dataclass
class Member:
    id: int
    email: str
    password_hash: str
    created: datetime
    email_verified: datetime | None
    last_totp: str | None
    totp_secret: str | None
```

We now also need to update the following model functions in *backend/src/backend/models/member.py*:

```python
async def select_member_by_email(
    db: Connection, email: str
) -> Member | None:
    result = await db.fetch_one(
        """SELECT id, email, password_hash, created,
                email_verified, last_totp, totp_secret
            FROM members
            WHERE LOWER(email) = LOWER(:email)""",
        {"email": email},
    )
    return None if result is None else Member(**result)


async def select_member_by_id(
    db: Connection, id: int
) -> Member | None:
    result = await db.fetch_one(
        """SELECT id, email, password_hash, created,
                email_verified, last_totp, totp_secret
            FROM members
            WHERE id = :id""",
        {"id": id},
    )
    return None if result is None else Member(**result)
```

```
async def insert_member(
    db: Connection, email: str, password_hash: str
) -> Member:
    result = await db.fetch_one(
        """INSERT INTO members (email, password_hash)
                VALUES (:email, :password_hash)
            RETURNING id, email, password_hash, created,
                      email_verified, last_totp,
                      totp_secret""",
        {"email": email, "password_hash": password_hash},
    )
    return Member(**result)
```

Note that the only change (as highlighted) is to add the new columns to the SQL query.

To be able to change the values of the last_totp and totp_secret columns, we'll need to add the following functions to *backend/src/backend/models/member.py*:

```
async def update_totp_secret(
    db: Connection, id: int, totp_secret: str | None
) -> None:
    await db.execute(
        """UPDATE members
              SET totp_secret = :totp_secret
            WHERE id = :id""",
        {"id": id, "totp_secret": totp_secret},
    )


async def update_last_totp(
    db: Connection, id: int, last_totp: str | None
) -> None:
    await db.execute(
        """UPDATE members
              SET last_totp = :last_totp
            WHERE id = :id""",
        {"id": id, "last_totp": last_totp},
    )
```

With the database and backend models updated, we can add the functionality to activate MFA.

Activating MFA

To activate MFA, we will need a page in our app that follows the process shown in *Figure 7.1*:

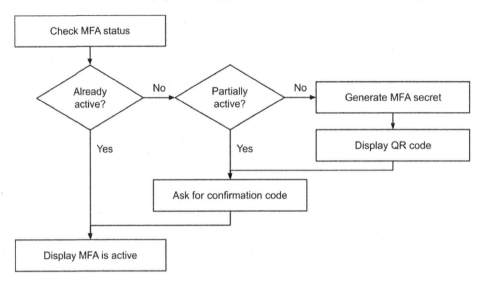

Figure 7.1: MFA activation process

The secret itself will need to be generated and managed on the backend, which we can do using the `pyotp` library; the library is installed by running the following in the *backend* directory:

```
pdm add pyotp
```

We can now start adding the backend routes, beginning with a route that returns the member's MFA status. This will either be `active` where MFA is in use, `inactive` where MFA is not in use, or `partial` where the member is in the process of activating MFA; it will also need to return the shared secret. We'll return the secret as a URI from which we can generate a QR code.

The code for this route is as follows and should be added to *backend/src/backend/blueprints/members.py*:

```
from typing import Literal

from pyotp.totp import TOTP
from quart_schema import validate_response

@dataclass
```

```python
class TOTPData:
    state: Literal["ACTIVE", "PARTIAL", "INACTIVE"]
    totp_uri: str | None


@blueprint.get("/members/mfa/")
@rate_limit(10, timedelta(seconds=10))
@login_required
@validate_response(TOTPData)
async def get_mfa_status() -> TOTPData:
    member_id = int(cast(str, current_user.auth_id))
    member = await select_member_by_id(g.connection, member_id)
    assert member is not None  # nosec
    totp_uri = None

    state: Literal["ACTIVE", "PARTIAL", "INACTIVE"]
    if member.totp_secret is None:
        state = "INACTIVE"
    elif (
        member.totp_secret is not None and
        member.last_totp is None
    ):
        totp_uri = TOTP(member.totp_secret).provisioning_uri(
            member.email, issuer_name="Tozo"
        )
        state = "PARTIAL"
    else:
        state = "ACTIVE"

    return TOTPData(state=state, totp_uri=totp_uri)
```

Note that `totp_uri` is only returned for a partial state (highlighted), as the secret it contains should only be shared when it is needed.

The next route we need is to allow a member to initiate MFA, by creating a shared secret. This should be added to *backend/src/backend/blueprints/members.py*:

```python
from pyotp import random_base32

from backend.models.member import update_totp_secret

@blueprint.post("/members/mfa/")
@rate_limit(10, timedelta(seconds=10))
@login_required
@validate_response(TOTPData)
async def initiate_mfa() -> TOTPData:
    member_id = int(cast(str, current_user.auth_id))
    member = await select_member_by_id(g.connection, member_id)
    assert member is not None    # nosec

    if member.totp_secret is not None:
        raise APIError(409, "ALREADY_ACTIVE")

    totp_secret = random_base32()
    totp_uri = TOTP(totp_secret).provisioning_uri(
        member.email, issuer_name="Tozo"
    )
    await update_totp_secret(g.connection, member_id, totp_
      secret)
    return TOTPData(state="PARTIAL", totp_uri=totp_uri)
```

The final route we need is to confirm the setup by allowing the user to put a TOTP code, which should be added to *backend/src/backend/blueprints/members.py*:

```python
from backend.models.member import update_last_totp

@dataclass
class TOTPToken:
    token: str

@blueprint.put("/members/mfa/")
@rate_limit(10, timedelta(seconds=10))
```

```
@login_required
@validate_request(TOTPToken)
async def confirm_mfa(data: TOTPToken) -> ResponseReturnValue:
    member_id = int(cast(str, current_user.auth_id))
    member = await select_member_by_id(g.connection, member_id)
    assert member is not None  # nosec

    if member.totp_secret is None:
        raise APIError(409, "NOT_ACTIVE")

    totp = TOTP(member.totp_secret)
    if totp.verify(data.token):
        await update_last_totp(g.connection, member_id, data.
          token)
        return {}
    else:
        raise APIError(400, "INVALID_TOKEN")
```

We can now build the frontend page to handle the interface, which will need to display a QR code. We can do that via qrcode.react, which is installed by running the following command in the *frontend* directory:

npm install qrcode.react

The page we need to build should look like *Figure 7.2*:

Figure 7.2: The MFA setup page

To build the MFA page, we first need to add a specific field for the user to enter one-time codes, by adding the following to *frontend/src/components/TotpField.tsx*:

```
import TextField, { TextFieldProps } from "@mui/material/
TextField";
import { FieldHookConfig, useField } from "formik";

import { combineHelperText } from "src/utils";

const TotpField = (props: FieldHookConfig<string> &
TextFieldProps) => {
  const [field, meta] = useField<string>(props);

  return (
    <TextField
      {...props}
      autoComplete="one-time-code"
      error={Boolean(meta.error) && meta.touched}
      helperText={combineHelperText(props.helperText, meta)}
      inputProps={{ inputMode: "numeric", maxLength: 6,
        pattern: "[0-9]*" }}
      margin="normal"
      type="text"
      {...field}
    />
  );
};

export default TotpField;
```

Before we use `TotpField`, we need to add the functionality required to activate MFA to *frontend/src/pages/MFA.tsx*:

```
import axios from "axios";
import { useQueryClient } from "@tanstack/react-query";

import { useMutation } from "src/query";
```

```
const useActivateMFA = (): [() => Promise<void>, boolean] => {
  const queryClient = useQueryClient();

  const { mutateAsync: activate, isLoading } = useMutation(
    async () => await axios.post("/members/mfa/"),
    {
      onSuccess: () => queryClient.invalidateQueries(["mfa"]),
    },
  );

  return [
    async () => {
      await activate();
    },
    isLoading,
  ];
};
```

The mutation invalidates the `mfa` queries, as this is the key that we'll use for the query that determines the user's MFA state.

We also need functionality to confirm the MFA activation, which can be added to *frontend/src/pages/MFA.tsx*:

```
import { FormikHelpers } from "formik";
import { useContext } from "react";

import { ToastContext } from "src/ToastContext";

interface IForm {
  token: string;
}

const useConfirmMFA = () => {
  const { addToast } = useContext(ToastContext);
  const queryClient = useQueryClient();

  const { mutateAsync: confirm } = useMutation(
```

```
      async (data: IForm) => await axios.put("/members/mfa/",
data),
    {
      onSuccess: () => queryClient.invalidateQueries(["mfa"]),
    },
  );


  return async (
    data: IForm, { setFieldError }: FormikHelpers<IForm>
  ) => {
    try {
      await confirm(data);
    } catch (error: any) {
      if (axios.isAxiosError(error) &&
          error.response?.status === 400) {
        setFieldError("token", "Invalid code");
      } else {
        addToast("Try again", "error");
      }
    }
  };
};
```

With the functionality in place, we can add the UI elements, as follows, which should be added to *frontend/src/pages/MFA.tsx*:

```
import LoadingButton from "@mui/lab/LoadingButton";
import Skeleton from "@mui/material/Skeleton";
import Typography from "@mui/material/Typography";
import { Form, Formik } from "formik";
import { QRCodeSVG } from "qrcode.react";
import * as yup from "yup";

import FormActions from "src/components/FormActions";
import Title from "src/components/Title";
import TotpField from "src/components/TotpField";
import { useQuery } from "src/query";
```

```
const validationSchema = yup.object({
  token: yup.string().required("Required"),
});

const MFA = () => {
  const { data } = useQuery(["mfa"], async () => {
    const response = await axios.get("/members/mfa/");
    return response.data;
  });
  const [activate, isLoading] = useActivateMFA();
  const onSubmit = useConfirmMFA();

  let content = <Skeleton />;
  if (data?.state === "ACTIVE") {
    content = <Typography variant="body1">MFA Active</
Typography>;
  } else if (data?.state === "INACTIVE") {
    content = (
      <LoadingButton loading={isLoading} onClick={activate}>
        Activate
      </LoadingButton>
    );
  } else if (data !== undefined) {
    content = (
      <>
        <QRCodeSVG value={data.totpUri} />
        <Formik<IForm>
          initialValues={{ token: "" }}
          onSubmit={onSubmit}
          validationSchema={validationSchema}
        >
          {(({ dirty, isSubmitting }) => (
            <Form>
              <TotpField
                fullWidth={true}
```

```
                    label="One time code"
                    name="token"
                    required={true}
                />
                <FormActions
                    disabled={!dirty}
                    isSubmitting={isSubmitting}
                    label="Confirm"
                    links={[{ label: "Back", to: "/" }]}
                />
            </Form>
        )}
        </Formik>
    </>
    );
}


return (
    <>
        <Title title="Multi-Factor Authentication" />
        {content}
    </>
    );
};


export default MFA;
```

The displayed UI code is dependent on the MFA state, including initially when a `Skeleton` is shown while the MFA state is being fetched from the backend. It then shows a `LoadingButton` to activate MFA, a QR code and `TotpField` to confirm MFA activation, and finally confirmation text if MFA is active.

Next, the MFA page needs to be added to the routing by adding the following to *frontend/src/Router.tsx*:

```
import MFA from "src/pages/MFA";


const Router = () => (
    <BrowserRouter>
```

```
    ...
    <Routes>
      ...
      <Route
        path="/mfa/"
        element={<RequireAuth><MFA /></RequireAuth>}
      />
    </Routes>
  </BrowserRouter>
);
```

In the code block, . . . represents code that has been omitted for brevity.

To allow the user to find the MFA page, we can add the following MenuItem to the AccountMenu component in *frontend/src/components/AccountMenu.tsx*:

```
<MenuItem
    component={Link}
    onClick={onMenuClose}
    to="/mfa/"
>
    MFA
</MenuItem>
```

Now that the user can activate MFA, we can utilize it in the login process.

Logging in with MFA

The login process must also change to ask the user for a one-time code if they have activated MFA. To do this, the backend must indicate to the frontend that an additional token is required for users that have activated MFA. The following code should replace the login route in *backend/src/backend/blueprints/sessions.py*:

```
from pyotp.totp import TOTP

from backend.models.member import update_last_totp

@dataclass
class LoginData:
    email: EmailStr
```

```
    password: str
    remember: bool = False
    token: str | None = None


@blueprint.post("/sessions/")
@rate_limit(5, timedelta(minutes=1))
@validate_request(LoginData)
async def login(data: LoginData) -> ResponseReturnValue:
    member = await select_member_by_email(g.connection, data.
email)
    password_hash = REFERENCE_HASH
    if member is not None:
        password_hash = member.password_hash

    passwords_match = bcrypt.checkpw(
        data.password.encode("utf-8"),
        password_hash.encode("utf-8"),
    )
    if passwords_match:
        assert member is not None  # nosec
        if (
            member.totp_secret is not None and
            member.last_totp is not None
        ):
            if data.token is None:
                raise APIError(400, "TOKEN_REQUIRED")

            totp = TOTP(member.totp_secret)
            if (
                not totp.verify(data.token) or
                data.token == member.last_totp
            ):
                raise APIError(401, "INVALID_CREDENTIALS")

            await update_last_totp(
                g.connection, member.id, data.token
```

```
        )

        login_user(AuthUser(str(member.id)), data.remember)
        return {}, 200
    else:
        raise APIError(401, "INVALID_CREDENTIALS")
```

This code will return a 400 error response if the user has activated MFA, but the login data doesn't include a one-time code (token); this allows the frontend login page to then ask the user for the one-time code and then retry logging in. In addition, the code will return a 401 invalid credentials message if the one-time code is invalid – noting that it checks the previously used code to prevent replay attacks.

We can now alter the existing login page so that it looks like *Figure 7.3* for accounts that have activated MFA:

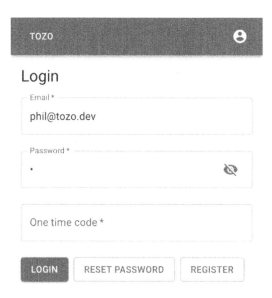

Figure 7.3: The Login page with the additional One time code field

To begin, we need to alter the useLogin logic in *frontend/src/pages/Login.tsx* to be the following:

```
import { useState } from "react";

interface IForm {
  email: string;
```

```
    password: string;
    token: string;
}

const useLogin = (): [(data: IForm, helpers:
FormikHelpers<IForm>) => Promise<void>, boolean] => {
  const [requiresMFA, setRequiresMFA] = useState(false);
  const location = useLocation();
  const navigate = useNavigate();
  const { addToast } = useContext(ToastContext);
  const { setAuthenticated } = useContext(AuthContext);
  const { mutateAsync: login } = useMutation(
    async (data: IForm) => await axios.post("/sessions/",
      data),
  );

  return [
    async (data: IForm, { setFieldError }:
      FormikHelpers<IForm>)=>{
      const loginData: any = {
        email: data.email,
        password: data.password,
      };
      if (requiresMFA) {
        loginData["token"] = data.token;
      }
      try {
        await login(loginData);
        setAuthenticated(true);
        navigate((location.state as any)?.from ?? "/");
      } catch (error: any) {
        if (error.response?.status === 400) {
          setRequiresMFA(true);
        } else if (error.response?.status === 401) {
          setFieldError("email", "Invalid credentials");
          setFieldError("password", "Invalid credentials");
          setFieldError("token", "Invalid credentials");
```

```
            } else {
                addToast("Try again", "error");
            }
        }
    },
    requiresMFA,
  ];
};
```

The `useLogin` hook returns the login functionality and a flag indicating whether a one-time code is required. This flag is set when a login is attempted, and a 400 response is returned by the backend.

We can use the flag from the `useLogin` hook to show `TotpField` in the login form by making the highlighted changes to *frontend/src/pages/Login.tsx*:

```
import TotpField from "src/components/TotpField";

const Login = () => {
  const [onSubmit, requiresMFA] = useLogin();
  ...

  return (
    <>
      <Formik<IForm>
        initialValues={{
          email: (location.state as any)?.email ?? "",
          password: "",
          token: "",
        }}
        onSubmit={onSubmit}
        validationSchema={validationSchema}
      >
        {({ isSubmitting, values }) => (
          <Form>
            {requiresMFA ? (
              <TotpField
                fullWidth={true}
                label="One time code"
```

```
                name="token"
                required={true}
            />
        ) : null}
      </Form>
    )}
  </Formik>
  </>
);
};
```

This will allow the user to type in a one-time code and complete the login. We can now consider how to handle the user losing the shared secret.

Recovering and inactivating MFA

Users will inevitably lose the shared secret and need to recover access to their accounts. This is something that is often done via recovery codes that the user is given when activating MFA. These recovery codes are additional single-use secrets stored in the backend and can be used once to regain access. While this works, any recovery system needs to consider how and what form your customer service will take, as users typically reach out for help.

OWASP provides additional guidance for this, which you can see here: `cheatsheetseries.owasp.org/cheatsheets/Multifactor_Authentication_Cheat_Sheet.html#resetting-mfa`.

We've successfully made a major change to our app, which you can use as a template for further major changes you'll need to make for your app. Next, we package our app for the app stores by converting it into a progressive web app.

Converting to a Progressive Web App

We can make our app more user-friendly, especially on mobile devices, by converting it into a **progressive web app** (**PWA**). PWAs can be installed on a mobile, like all other apps, either via the app stores or directly from a prompt in the browser. PWAs can also work offline and use other advanced features such as push notifications. However, PWAs are more complicated to develop, and service workers (a key feature) can be very difficult to get right.

> **Service workers**
>
> Service workers are custom JavaScript scripts that act as a proxy between the web page and the server. This allows the service worker to add offline-frst functionality, such as caching pages for performance or accepting push notifications.

A PWA must have a service worker and a manifest file to work; these are available via the `create-react-app` tool we used in *Chapter 1, Setting Up Our System for Development*. To do so, let's create a new `react` app using the PWA template in a temporary directory:

```
npx create-react-app temp --template cra-template-pwa-
typescript
```

We can then copy the service worker code from this temporary project into ours by copying the following files:

- Copy *temp/src/service-worker.ts* to *frontend/src/service-worker.ts*

- Copy *temp/src/serviceWorkerRegistration.ts* to *frontend/src/serviceWorkerRegistration.ts*

The *temp* directory can now be deleted or kept for reference if you prefer.

To activate the service worker, the following should be added to *frontend/src/index.tsx* to register the service worker:

```
import * as serviceWorkerRegistration from "src/
serviceWorkerRegistration";

serviceWorkerRegistration.register();
```

This service worker needs a large number of dependencies from the workbox toolkit (`web.dev/workbox/`) to work; these dependencies are developed by Google to make service workers easier to use. These dependencies can be installed by running the following in the *frontend* directory:

```
npm install workbox-background-sync workbox-background-sync
workbox-cacheable-response workbox-core workbox-expiration
workbox-navigation-preload workbox-precaching workbox-range-
requests workbox-routing workbox-strategies workbox-streams
```

The service worker isn't active while we develop the app using the frontend development server with `npm run start`, so to test it, we need to serve it locally by the backend development server. First, we must build the frontend, by running the following in the *frontend* directory:

```
npm run build
```

This will have created files in the *frontend/build* directory, which we need to copy over to the backend. This requires the following file movements:

- Copy the entire *frontend/build/static* directory to *backend/src/backend/static*

- Copy the *frontend/build/index.html* file to *backend/src/backend/templates/index.html*

- Copy the remaining files in *frontend/build* to *backend/src/backend/static* (e.g., *frontend/build/service-worker.js* to *backend/src/backend/static/service-worker.js*)

The remaining files also need to be included in *Dockerfile*, and the following should be added next to the existing COPY --from=frontend commands:

```
COPY --from=frontend /frontend/build/*.js* /app/backend/static/
```

With the backend running (via pdm run start), the service worker-enabled app is reachable at localhost:5050. You can check the service worker is working via the dev tools console as seen in *Figure 7.4*:

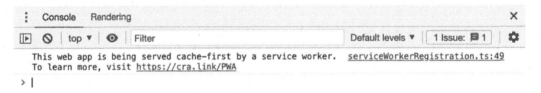

Figure 7.4: The service worker output in the browser dev tools

The service worker will now start caching the content, and you should be able to refresh the app while the backend is not running.

App icons

Web pages in the browser have an icon associated with them, typically shown next to the title in the tab. This icon is called the favicon. A PWA has additional icons used for the app on the mobile home screen (and elsewhere); these icons are defined in the manifest file.

We can now turn our attention to the manifest file, which describes the app and the logo that should be associated with it. Once you have designed a logo, I'd recommend that it be saved as a favicon in the SVG format placed in *frontend/public/favicon.svg*. As we are using an SVG format rather than ICO, the following should replace the existing code in *frontend/public/index.html* (note the file extension):

```
<link rel="icon" href="%PUBLIC_URL%/favicon.svg" />
```

The same logo then needs to be saved in the PNG format as a 192x192 pixel square in *frontend/public/logo192.png* and as a 512x512 pixel square in *frontend/public/logo512.png*. The manifest should include the following, which should be placed in *frontend/public/manifest.json*:

```json
{
    "short_name": "Tozo",
    "name": "Tozo todo app",
    "icons": [
        {
            "src": "favicon.svg",
            "sizes": "64x64 32x32 24x24 16x16",
            "type": " image/svg+xml"
        },
        {
            "src": "logo192.png",
            "type": "image/png",
            "sizes": "192x192"
        },
        {
            "src": "logo512.png",
            "type": "image/png",
            "sizes": "512x512"
        }
    ],
    "start_url": ".",
    "display": "standalone",
    "theme_color": "#1976d2",
    "background_color": "#ffffff"
}
```

As with the service worker, we also need to copy the logos to the backend. For development, copy all the logos to the *backend/src/backend/static/* folder. For production, the following should be added to the *Dockerfile*:

```
COPY --from=frontend /frontend/build/*.png /frontend/build/*.
svg /app/backend/static/
```

We now need to serve these new files from the backend, which we can do by adding the following code to *backend/src/backend/blueprints/serving.py*:

```
from quart import current_app, send_from_directory


@blueprint.get(
    "/<any('service-worker.js', 'service-worker.js.map',
'manifest.json', 'asset-manifest.json', 'favicon.svg',
'logo192.png', 'logo512.png'):path>"  # noqa: E501
)
@rate_exempt
async def resources(path: str) -> ResponseReturnValue:
    assert current_app.static_folder is not None  # nosec
    return await send_from_directory(
        current_app.static_folder, path
    )
```

With these changes made, our app is a PWA, which means that we can package it for the app stores. The easiest way to do so is to use `pwabuilder.com`, which will create iOS and Android packages. To do so, visit `pwabuilder.com` and enter your app's domain. It will then present the packages that can be uploaded to the Google Play store and iOS app stores.

PWA Builder
PWA Builder is a Microsoft-directed project to improve PWA adoption by making it easier. PWAs are first-class apps on Windows and Android.

There are limitations to this approach; first, while PWAs are first-class apps on Windows and Android systems, they have limited support on Apple's iOS. It may be the case that your app as packaged by PWA Builder is not accepted on the app store – with little explanation why. In addition, iOS does not support all the features that PWAs can; the most notable being that push notifications will not be supported till 2023.

With the conversion to PWA complete, we can upload the PWA package to the various app stores allowing users to install it on their phones from the store. Further instructions on how to do so are given for Android (`https://docs.pwabuilder.com/#/builder/android`) and iOS (`https://docs.pwabuilder.com/#/builder/app-store`).

Summary

In this chapter, we've secured our app and adopted a process of continual updates to keep it secure. We've also added a major feature, MFA, which will serve as a guide for making future major changes to your app. Finally, we've packaged our app ready to be added to the app stores.

This is a great place to be, as you now have a blueprint for a web app that is running in production using many industry best practices. This is a blueprint you can adapt for your own needs with the to-do specific aspects serving as a guide, and I hope that the best practices and tools I've introduced to you serve you well.

Further reading

This isn't the end; there is much more you can and should now do to improve your app to make it more valuable to your users. I'd recommend you add more testing to reduce bugs, specifically by adding end-to-end testing. I'd also recommend you use tools such as Lighthouse, `pagespeed.web.dev`, to identify common performance, accessibility, and general PWA issues.

Index

Symbols

A

B

C

Packt.com

Subscribe to our online digital library for full access to over 7,000 books and videos, as well as industry leading tools to help you plan your personal development and advance your career. For more information, please visit our website.

Why subscribe?

- Spend less time learning and more time coding with practical eBooks and Videos from over 4,000 industry professionals

- Improve your learning with Skill Plans built especially for you

- Get a free eBook or video every month

- Fully searchable for easy access to vital information

- Copy and paste, print, and bookmark content

Did you know that Packt offers eBook versions of every book published, with PDF and ePub files available? You can upgrade to the eBook version at packt.com and as a print book customer, you are entitled to a discount on the eBook copy. Get in touch with us at customercare@packtpub.com for more details.

At www.packt.com, you can also read a collection of free technical articles, sign up for a range of free newsletters, and receive exclusive discounts and offers on Packt books and eBooks.

Other Books You May Enjoy

If you enjoyed this book, you may be interested in these other books by Packt:

Python Web Development with Sanic

Adam Hopkins

ISBN: 978-1-80181-441-6

- Understand the difference between WSGI, Async, and ASGI servers.
- Discover how Sanic organizes incoming data, why it does it, and how to make the most of it.
- Implement best practices for building reliable, performant, and secure web apps.
- Explore useful techniques for successfully testing and deploying a Sanic web app.
- Create effective solutions for the modern web, including task management, bot integration, and GraphQL.

Django 4 for the Impatient

Greg Lim | Daniel Correa

ISBN: 978-1-80324-583-6

- Understand and implement Django Apps' basic structure, including URLs, views, templates, and models
- Add bootstrap to improve the aesthetics of the site
- Create your own custom pages and have different URLs to route to them
- Navigate between pages by adding a header bar to all pages
- Work with databases and models

Packt is searching for authors like you

If you're interested in becoming an author for Packt, please visit `authors.packtpub.com` and apply today. We have worked with thousands of developers and tech professionals, just like you, to help them share their insight with the global tech community. You can make a general application, apply for a specific hot topic that we are recruiting an author for, or submit your own idea.

Share Your Thoughts

Now you've finished *A Blueprint for Production-Ready Web Applications*, we'd love to hear your thoughts! Scan the QR code below to go straight to the Amazon review page for this book and share your feedback or leave a review on the site that you purchased it from.

https://packt.link/r/1-803-24850-5

Your review is important to us and the tech community and will help us make sure we're delivering excellent quality content.

Made in United States
North Haven, CT
27 May 2023

37040232R00157